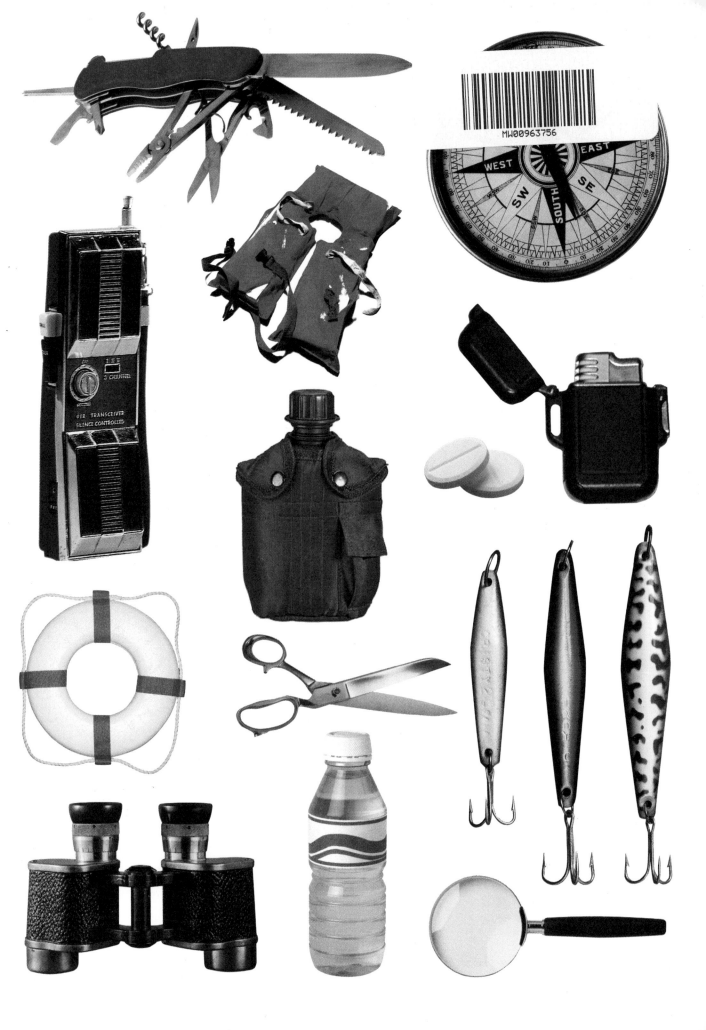

People

AMAZING STORIES OF SURVIVAL
TALES OF HOPE, HEROISM & ASTOUNDING LUCK

CONTENTS

LIVING TO TELL THE TALE

THERE IS NOTHING more exhilarating," Winston Churchill once wrote, "than to be shot at without result."

No doubt. Most of us, however, are quite willing to make do with reading about *other* people who have been shot at—or frozen on Everest, lost at sea for 144 days, chased by a machete-swinging madman, clamped in the jaws of a mountain lion or hit by lightning—and lived to tell the tale. Over the years, PEOPLE has published scores of such stories; this book contains 50 of the best.

What's the draw? Probably that the narrative of a survival story is, by its nature, dramatic (a charging elephant will almost always hold the reader's attention). Also, survival stories give us hope ("If *that* guy lived though a plane crash/shipwreck/fall into a soybean silo, maybe I could too").

And—no small thing—they make us grateful. Over and over, the survivors in this book say the same thing: When you're caught in a crisis, confronting a horrible fate head on, there is nothing so exhilarating as finding yourself—suddenly, almost inexplicably, even, it may seem, miraculously—*alive*.

THAT'S INCREDIBLE

GRABBED BY A GATOR, FROZEN ON EVEREST, FALLING THREE MILES WITHOUT A PARACHUTE: 10 I-CAN'T-BELIEVE-THEY-DID-THAT TALES

DEAD MAN CLIMBING

Covered in snow and left to die, Beck Weathers woke up, climbed down Mount Everest and emerged alone from a storm that claimed eight lives

Weathers (above) was upbeat before setting out on his near-fatal climb. At the time, he said later, "I had this idea that a person's accomplishments were what defined him. Today, I'm a lot more at peace with myself. I no longer feel a need to come up with new things to challenge myself."

SEABORN BECK WEATHERS, *a Dallas pathologist, was 49 when he joined a 1996 expedition planning to climb Mount Everest. That year, a freak storm caught dozens of mountaineers high on Everest's south face; eight died in a matter of hours, a tragedy documented in John Krakauer's 1997 bestseller,* Into Thin Air.

Weathers was almost one of them. Exhausted and snowblind, he had collapsed while trying to get back to camp. "I thought Weathers was dead," said Stuart Hutchinson, a Canadian climber who found Weathers's body half buried in snow. "I unburied him and broke the ice off his face."

But Beck Weathers wasn't dead.

On May 5, after a month of acclimating to the altitude (Everest's base camps are 18,000 ft. above sea level), Weathers, team leader Rob Hall and eight others made the six-day climb to the high camp, 28,000 feet up Everest's south slope. Like the others, Hall's team rested there for a few hours, then set out for the top at midnight, the path lit by the glow of their headlamps.

At first, Weathers led the way. "I was at the head of the pack," he says. But when his vision began to blur—perhaps a result of an airborne ice splinter—he fell back in line. When the group reached the Southeast Ridge just before dawn, Weathers was nearly, though temporarily, blind. Only 400 feet from the summit, he made the painful decision to wait until his vision cleared or until descending climbers could steer him back to the high camp. Hall, who didn't like to see his group divided, made Weathers promise to wait until he could lead him down personally. "I made him that promise," says Weathers. "I had no choice."

The morning was windy but clear, a near-perfect summit day, and eventually climbers started making their way back to camp. When teammate Jon Krakauer found Weathers on the ridge, he told him Hall was at least three hours behind but that climbers Yasuko Namba and Mike Groom, who were carrying a radio, were just 20 minutes upslope. Weathers decided to wait for them

and then radio Hall that he was descending. "That 20 minutes was fateful," Weathers later said.

Minutes after Krakauer left, wind gusts swelled into a gale, and snow began to fall. By the time Namba and Groom reached Weathers, the temperature had plummeted to minus 4 and visibility was almost nil. As darkness neared, Americans Tim

Madsen, Charlotte Fox and Sandy Hill Pittman joined the trio to begin edging down the mountain. "We formed into a tight pack, forcing everyone to stay awake, to keep moving," says Weathers. "You would slap each other on the back, anything to keep movement going and make sure no one fell asleep."

Feeling his right hand going numb, Weathers took off his glove and put his hand beneath his jacket to try to warm it. Disastrously, he lost his grip, and the glove vanished into the night. With it went the last of Weathers's strength. "I remember the voices getting dim, faint, far away," he says. His already blurred vision dimming, his knees buckling, he lay down in the snow. From that moment, he doesn't remember anything.

During the next 24 hours, the storm claimed eight climbers, including team leader Hall, who managed to make a heartbreaking call from near the top of Everest before he died. Via the small satellite phone he was carrying, he was

"We knew what we were doing," said Weathers (back row, third from right, with his team before their attempted ascent of Everest, above). "What happened was a total surprise."

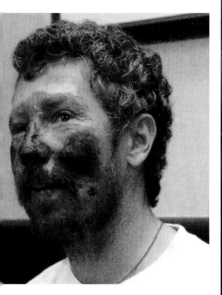

He lost part of his nose and his hands, but, says Weathers (with his wife, Peach), "I was not ready to give up life or my family."

able to contact his wife in New Zealand to tell her he was trapped but also to try to reassure her that he would be okay. Weathers had been lying still for hours when climber Stuart Hutchinson found him, broke the ice off his frozen face and concluded he was dead.

The grim news was relayed to base camp, then to New Zealand and, finally, in a 7:15 a.m. call to Beck's wife, Peach Weathers, in Dallas. "I have terrible news," Hall's assistant told her. At first, Peach didn't get it. "You mean he's missing?" she asked. No, her husband was dead. His body had been identified. Still in shock, Peach phoned friends and her husband's brother Dan, 47. "I started thinking about whether they would be able to retrieve his body," she says. Mostly, Peach wondered how she would tell their three children their father had died.

Meanwhile, on the mountain, Weathers woke up. He was disoriented, with ice on his face and his right hand frozen like a rock, but he was, to his surprise, alive. Gradually grasping his situation, he began thinking about his wife and children—"the things I wouldn't be able to say to them"—and found the strength to get to his feet. Near blind and staggering, he pushed through the snow, eventually coming to the blue tents of the high camp, where astonished climbers rushed to his side. They cut the frozen clothes from his body, gave

"We formed into a tight pack, forcing everyone to stay awake, to keep moving. You would slap each other on the back, anything to keep movement going"

him oxygen and warmed him with a hot water bottle.

They also radioed that he had survived. Three hours after Peach heard her husband had perished, she received another phone call. This time, to her great relief, she was told he was in critical condition but alive.

After another stormy night, when the tents nearly blew off the mountain, the badly weakened Weathers continued down in the company of climbers Pete Athans and Todd Burleson. Two days later, after they reached Camp 1, Weathers and another frostbitten climber, Makalu Gau, 39, were rescued by a Nepalese-army helicopter pilot, who braved high winds and dangerously thin air to carry them to safety.

Bandaged and warm, lying in a

Kathmandu hotel hours later, Weathers reflected on how close he had come to dying. "I was looking out the window at all the greenery, and the fact I was still alive really overcame me," he says. "I can't tell you the euphoria I felt."

He had suffered terribly. Doctors later amputated his right arm below the elbow, as well as the fingers of his left hand. They used his own tissues to fashion a new nose to replace the one that had been so severely frostbitten. In all, he says, it is a small price to pay for the privilege of being alive. "All those things I worried I'd never get the chance to say to my wife and kids," he adds, "I've had the opportunity to say." Smiling at her husband, Peach offers, "The kids and I have suggested that Beck now take up bass fishing."

FIRST, HE SAW THE FIN

Krishna Thompson felt a powerful crunch. "I can't believe there's a shark on my leg," he thought. Then he punched it in the nose

IT SEEMED AN IDEAL WAY *for Krishna Thompson and his wife, AveMaria, to celebrate their 10th anniversary: a trip to Grand Bahama Island. On Aug. 4, 2001, the first morning of their vacation, Thompson, 40, a New York City banker, went out for an early swim. It was relaxing and peaceful—at first.*

I had swum out about 20 feet and was treading water looking out toward the ocean. That's when I saw it—the shark fin speeding straight for me. I tried throwing my body toward the shore. I thought I'd get out of his way. I'm a quick guy, but the shark hit my right leg. Then he caught my left leg, and I heard his teeth go into the bone.

He towed me out into the ocean; he just kept going, and I was thinking, "I can't believe there's a shark on my leg." The water was frigid. I think that's why I felt pressure but no pain. I thought about my wife and how we didn't even have children yet. I thought, "I'm going to die." I remember saying aloud, "Oh God, get me out of this."

I tried to get free by throwing my body around. But the grip was awesome. Then he took me under. I remember the swirling, like when water goes down a drain; the daylight disappeared into that little hole. That's when he began violently shaking me like a rag doll. Time was running out.

It was dark. I just tried to imagine where its mouth was, felt around and pulled it open. I got free—I couldn't believe it. Then I gave the shark two quick blows to the nose—one, two—and it just swam away. All around me the water was red. As soon as I was clear of that shark, the first thing I did was look at my leg. All I saw was bone; no skin, no arteries.

I just started to swim. Once I reached shallow water I started hopping toward the beach. I tried to yell, but it wouldn't come out. Finally I reached deep down and screamed. That's when people came running. I wasn't feeling pain in the leg; I think all my nerves were gone. I couldn't move my good leg, arms or tongue. I kept fading, thinking it's a dream, and then I'd be like, "No, it's real. I can hear them working on me." My heart was pounding. Then it slowed, and I thought my body was shutting down.

I woke up in a Miami hospital, happy because I was alive. I didn't look to see the leg was amputated. I just knew. Someone asked if there was anything they could get me. I said, "How about a leg?"

I got one a month later—a computerized limb called a C-leg with a microprocessor in the knee that adjusts the way the leg flexes. It's the closest you can get to a real leg.

My daughter Indira was born on Sept. 26, 2002. To go from thinking you're going to die and not have children to watching your child born in front of you, it's the greatest thing. When you've been in the jaws of a shark and then you think about your worst day—there's no comparison.

A HOSTAGE FIGHTS BACK

Held at gunpoint by a bank robber, Paul Hardy saved his sons, then attacked the crook

ON FEB. 11, 1998, *Paul Hardy, a 32-year-old former jail guard employed by the Essex County (Mass.) Sheriff's Department, had just arrived home from his early-morning shift and was looking forward to a quiet afternoon with Kevin and Kyle, his 4-year-old twin sons. He didn't know that a masked gunman named Chad Austin had led police on a 56-mile high-speed chase after robbing a bank—or that Austin was about to suddenly enter his life.*

It was around 11:30 a.m., and I was just chilling with the kids, half asleep watching TV, when I heard a couple of bangs. I thought they might have been doing construction next door. Then I heard a real loud bang and glass shattering in the kitchen. And this guy, who'd just shot his way in through the sliding doors, runs into the living room wearing a ski mask

The final moments: Hardy (top row, far left) persuaded gunman Chad Austin (below) to let his sons go, and police whisked them to safety. Then Hardy attacked Austin (bottom row, far left) and leaped out the window to safety.

and pointing a gun. He's still looking behind him to see if the cops are chasing him. He turns around and sees me sitting there, groggy. "Get down," he says. "Get down."

Until then I was thinking, "This ain't happening. I must be half asleep." Then I knew this was a bad guy. I was like, "My God, this is real."

I scooped up the twins and did what he said. I asked him if I could put the kids in the corner. "Yeah, that's okay," he says. I set them up with a pillow and a blanket, and in a half hour they were sound asleep.

As Austin sat on my sofa, making me sit on the floor in front of him, he started counting the money he had dumped out of two pillowcases. "Look at all this that I'll never be able to spend," he says, peeking out the window. "I'm having a really bad day." I say, "Yeah, mine ain't much better."

After about 15 minutes, Austin picked up the cordless phone and called his parents. He left a message on their answering machine. By this point he knew the cops had the house surrounded. "I'm sorry the way things turned out," he says into the phone. "I really screwed up. I love you both. I'll see you on the other side."

My phone started ringing constantly, with friends who'd heard about the situation on TV. Then my wife's dentist called, and Austin took the message. "Your wife has an appointment at 9:30 tomorrow morning," he told me.

I'd had a few courses in hostage negotiations, and I was thinking about what they taught: Keep hostage takers talking, get personal, make them comfortable. When a news bulletin reported no cops had been killed, I told Austin that no matter how much he had screwed up, his parents and his wife loved him. "And you haven't killed any cops," I said. "There's light at the end of the tunnel."

Now two things came to mind. Either he was going to kill himself or he was going to run into the street and go out in a blaze of glory. "Don't worry," he says, "I won't do anything in front of your kids." I didn't feel so sure about that.

The whole time, I was thinking about my kids . . . focusing on how to solve this problem. Meanwhile, Austin was watching the live coverage. They reported that I worked for the sheriff's department, and I was worried he might get angrier. I was glad the kids were asleep. I kept thinking, "Daddy's going to die." He wanted to know where I kept my gun, and he didn't believe me when I told him I didn't keep one in the house because of the kids. He said, "I get chased by the cops going 130 miles per hour and getting shot at. And then, of all the houses, I break into a cop's house. I can't believe the day I'm having."

The police shut off the phone, and Austin was getting agitated. At about 4 p.m. he asked if I'd feel more comfortable with the kids out of the house. I was psyched—and relieved. I got them up and took them to the garage door.

Outside, there were dozens of police in SWAT gear behind cars and bushes. At first the boys didn't want to go. They said, "We want

you to come." Then Kevin ran to the SWAT team. But Kyle turned around and clung to my leg. "Kyle, you've got to go," I said. Finally, I just pushed him out and slammed the door. It was the hardest thing I've ever had to do.

I went back upstairs and sat in the rocking chair next to Austin. That way I could see what he was doing with the gun. I told him, "You can put the gun down now and walk out." He said there was no way he was going back to jail.

For the next 20 minutes nothing happened. Then I got this burning feeling in my gut. My heart was pounding. That's when I knew I was going to do something. "You bust into my house, you put a gun to me and my kids," I thought. "Enough is enough."

Not long after, I heard the dog walking on the broken glass in the kitchen. It sounded like someone was coming into the house, and Austin turned his head. "Screw it, now or never," I thought. And I jumped him and grabbed the gun with two hands. Two rounds went off, one through the couch; the other whizzed by my arm. "I'm going to kill you," he says. "No you're not," I say.

I gave him a head butt, and we rolled to the ground. I got the gun, and the magazine fell out. He started biting my hand and arm. Money was flying everywhere. Just as I was tiring, there was a boom and a flash of light as a police stun grenade exploded. I was dazed, but I stumbled to the window and leaped out.

What happened after that, I don't know. The SWAT team told me to get down, and I did because I didn't want to get shot by the good guys. They put me in the ambulance and checked me out. . . . After, I saw the kids and Gail. We hugged each other and sighed.

I'm still getting through the shock of it all. It scared the hell out of me. I'm just a regular guy who was backed into a corner and was able to save my kids.

Falling more than two miles to the ground taught Murray a valuable lesson: "I've learned to take time for the important things." Such as? "Saying 'I love you.'"

NO CHUTE? OH, SHOOT!

Skydiver Joan Murray fell 14,500 feet without a parachute—into a nest of fire ants

SEPT. 25, 1999 As the pilot leveled the plane off at 14,500 feet, Joan Murray took a final deep breath and leaped out the door. A bank exec from Charlotte, N.C., Murray always got a thrill when she jumped. This time, when she pulled the cord to release her parachute, nothing happened, and she felt a jolt of adrenaline like nothing she had ever felt before.

Dropping toward Earth at about 120 mph, Murray, 47, reached for the release to her reserve chute. It opened just fine, but Murray, in her confusion, spun out of control, causing the chute to deflate. Her descent had slowed briefly, but she continued to plunge toward the ground. "It wasn't one of my finer, brilliant moments," she said later.

Experts estimate that Murray was traveling about 80 mph when she hit the ground. The impact shattered the right side of her body and knocked fillings out of her teeth.

Then, unbelievably, things got worse. Murray had fallen into a mound of stinging fire ants, who were upset by the sudden intrusion. Swarming over the semiconscious Murray, they stung her more than 200 times before paramedics arrived. The good news, doctors theorized, was that the stings may have shocked her heart enough to keep it beating.

At the Carolinas Medical Center in Charlotte, Murray lay in a coma for two weeks, her 115-lb. body swelling from her injuries until she looked more than double her normal size. But six weeks later she was able to head home to continue her recovery. By June 2001, with a metal rod in her right leg and five 5-in. spikes in her pelvis, she limped back to work. She later experienced a short-term memory loss due to the impact with the ground. But the accident never dimmed her resolve. In July 2001, Murray passed a startling milestone, going up in a plane for her 37th skydive. "It was perfect," she said.

His leg gored and his pelvis crushed, Beard (top) endured a three-hour ride to an airstrip for evacuation. In a more peaceful moment (above), he conferred with his then-wife, model Cheryl Tiegs, in 1979.

PHOTOGRAPHER PETER BEARD, *onetime husband of model Cheryl Tiegs, may be best known for stylish images that light up the pages of the world's leading fashion magazines. But he is equally passionate about the wilderness. His 1965 book,* The End of the Game, *documented the starvation of thousands of elephants in a reserve in the native New Yorker's adopted home of Kenya. Given his affection for the majestic beasts, it was with pleasure that Beard, 59, accepted a friend's invitation to join him in early September 1996, on a safari to photograph elephants near the Kenyan border with Tanzania.*

CRUNCH TIME IN THE AFRICAN BUSH

An elephant charges, and a famous photographer
learns there's nowhere to hide

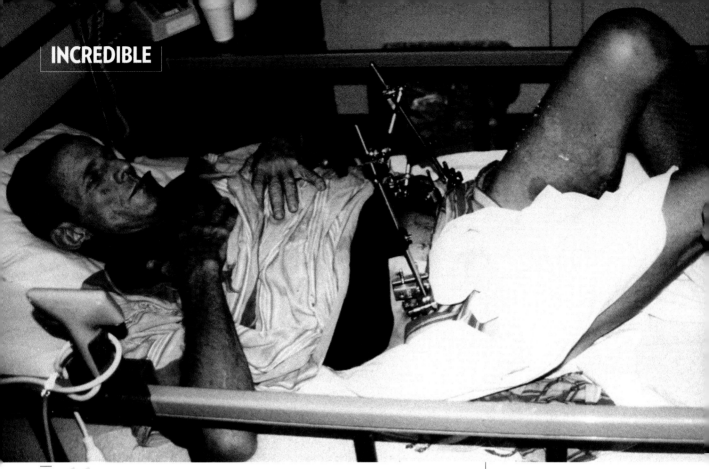

> " Crrrrr! Crrrrr! Broke my ribs. I was totally conscious. I could feel the whole pelvis going. It's like an elevator or a freight train coming down on you. Huge pressure"

All told, there were seven in our party, going on a picnic. My great friend Calvin Cottar and I had just gotten out of the car, and we were looking at this elephant. There were about 15 elephants 150 yards from us, ambling away. Typically, this matriarch turned around and gave us a demonstration charge—a warning. But her head was a little down, which was unusual. We ran back 50 to 100 feet just to make sure that a safe distance of around 150 yards was kept. We weren't even thinking. We were on automatic.

The moment the matriarch ended her charge, she rejoined the herd, and we saw that everything was okay. But then she turned around again and started coming at us. So we started running, looking over our shoulders, and it became obvious she was just not going to stop.

There was no cover, so I headed for an anthill, which was about three feet high, and I threw myself behind it. She came around it, and I managed to grab onto her left front leg. She did a couple of spins to knock me off. We're doing this little dance, and there were so many things going on that I don't really know what happened, but I think she pinned me against the anthill. Her tusk went right through my left thigh; there's a hole as big as my hand where it went in, but the hole on the other side is only about four inches. So I think the tusk went into the anthill, which is very hard, and that stopped it. Then she crushed me with her head.

It was just a steady crunching.

Crrrrr! Crrrrr! Broke my ribs. I was totally conscious. I could feel the whole pelvis going. It's like an elevator or a freight train coming down on you. Huge pressure, incredible pressure.

And then I lost my eyesight.

The rest of the herd came around,

and I lay there like a lump of flesh. She gave me this squish for maybe three to five seconds. I felt everything go pop, crunch, pop. I could hear all their feet. They usually trample you and make a grease spot out of you. But they totally left me alone—maybe because we had run so far away that they sensed we weren't their enemy.

About 10 seconds after they shuffled off, the car drove up, and Calvin came running over to me, screaming, "Take off your pants!" because he could see this huge hole. I thought it was a joke because I hadn't felt the tusk, just the squeezing. I said, "Listen, Calvin, not now. Not in front of all these people." It was noon, but I couldn't see a thing. It was completely black. I guess after about five minutes...my right eye cleared, then my left.

I said to Calvin, "Don't worry, I'm not going to sue." I was joking because I could tell by his voice he was really panicked. Then when I got my vision back and saw the hole in my leg, I was shocked. Thankfully, my artery was untouched.

We had one hell of a drive—three hours over rough Kenyan bush. We were on the radio the whole time trying to get help. We went about 20

"It took me a long time to be able to stand up," says Beard (left, awaiting surgery in New York). The incident did not dim his love of elephants, captured (right) in his book *The End of the Game.*

miles to an airstrip at Keekorok. Luckily we made radio contact with some people who got through to Nairobi. A medical plane came very quickly. Then I got a morphine shot, and that was the end of my real pain.

I arrived completely bled out at Nairobi Hospital and went right into the operating room. I had to have a lot of blood, six to eight pints. It was an "open book" fracture—my pelvis was split like you'd open a book—with about eight breaks all around. A surgeon there saved my life. He put in pins, drilled through the skin and attached them to an external steel frame to hold everything together.

After a second operation later to clean out the wound, they flew me via London to New York on Sept. 20. I was operated on again in St. Vincent's Hospital and Medical Center, where they took off the steel frame and put in titanium plates and screws. That operation lasted almost nine hours. I did a lot of physical therapy in New York and on Oct. 20 got out.

I'm a quick healer. . . . Now I can walk and just about run. There's no permanent damage, but I do have to continue therapy or I'll probably have arthritis in my pelvis and hips. And I've got a problem with the nerves in my left arm.

I'm not a sentimentalist, but I do feel I was very lucky. I have no problem with that elephant hitting me. I just thank God it didn't do a better job. Elephants are like humans. They are very smart, very logical. She owed human beings a real heavy debt, and she paid it to me. No elephant attacks like that unless it's been shot at or seen other elephants shot.

You've got to be more alert, because more animals have been pushed around, wounded, subjected to human harassment, ambushed, all kinds of stress. When they attack, it's totally predictable.

LION HEART

On Jan. 8, 2004, Anne Hjelle, 31, a personal trainer and ex-Marine, and her friend Debi Nicholls, 49, set out for a bike ride in Whiting Ranch Wilderness Park, not far from Hjelle's home in Mission Viejo, Calif. Suddenly, a shadow leapt from a bush . . .

"Anne [above] was 30 yards ahead of me," recalled her bike-riding partner, Nicholls. "I couldn't see her. Suddenly I heard screaming. As I came around the corner I saw this mountain lion. He was on top of her." The cat's other victim that day, cyclist Mark Reynolds, was the first to be killed by a mountain lion in California in 10 years.

AT ABOUT 4 P.M. Debi and I started up a one-way trail. After half an hour we took a narrow trail that was very fast, with a lot of blind corners—kind of like a roller coaster.

Suddenly, I saw a flash of reddish-brown fur over my right shoulder. An animal came out of the bushes and—Bam!—he grabbed my shoulders with his paws. I knew instantly it was a mountain lion. He latched on with his jaws to the back of my neck. "Jesus help me," I said. My first thought was to try to punch the lion. Having grown up with a dog, I figured if I could hit him in the nose, maybe he'd let go. As much as I tried, it seemed to have no effect.

A few seconds later, Debi rushed up and grabbed my leg. I was off the edge of the trail when the lion grabbed the left side of my face, one of his top fangs just below the bridge of my nose, the other into my upper lip. His bottom teeth were in my left cheek. As he closed down, I could feel my whole cheek tear away. I didn't feel pain. The lion did not make a sound. I remember thinking, "He just ripped my face off. I want to die." Then I thought of my husband. He and I are connected at the hip. I thought, "I have to make it."

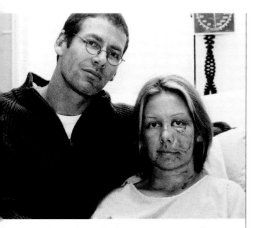

"Even though I have scars, I'm still Anne inside," said Hjelle (in the hospital with her husband, James Poindexter).

I was on my back and the lion was trying to get to the front of my throat. Debi held on to my leg, screaming for help, kicking at it. But the lion was determined—and finally he did get me by the front of my throat. When he clamped down, I could no longer breathe and I thought, "I'm going to die." I remember thinking, "Why don't I see my life flash before my eyes?" But I didn't. Instead, I passed out.

While Hjelle was unconscious, Nicholls continued to hold on as five male bikers responding to her cries arrived. After bikers pelted the lion with rocks, the animal gave way and took off. Two of the men helped Nicholls carry Hjelle up to the trail, while another phoned 911. Before help arrived, Hjelle came to.

It was like I was drowning in blood. I tried to breathe and was just gurgling. I thought if I could sit up, I might be able to get some air. Once I did, I thought, "I'm in the clear." It never occurred to me that I still might die. But I could feel my left cheek hanging like a flap. I could tell my left eye was messed up. But once I knew I could see out of it, I said to myself, "Okay, I can deal with this." When the firefighters showed up, I felt alert.

Hjelle was airlifted to Mission Hospital in Mission Viejo, where her husband, James Poindexter, 37, a kung fu instructor, raced to her side. Remarkably, she had suffered no internal injuries.

I'd lost blood but not enough to require a transfusion. The left side of my face was peeled away and connected only by my nose, which was broken, with damage to the left nostril. My left eye wasn't blinking. There was nerve damage, and most of the muscles on the lower eyelid were torn away. I had damage to nerve branches affecting movement of the lower eyelid and upper lip. There were deep puncture wounds in my neck. The trauma surgeon told me one wound went through tissue to the spinal column, but none of the wounds were life-threatening.

Hjelle underwent six hours of reconstructive surgery. Doctors also reconnected damaged nerves. The next day the bandages came off.

The first thing I did was ask for a mirror. I was shocked to see my looks completely changed. That was tough. The first time I walked down the hallway to the doctor's office, people stared. Guys look at women in a certain way, and now the stares were for a different reason. The thing is, I know my husband has unconditional love for me. I know he loves me for who I am, even with the scars.

Hjelle later learned that the mountain lion, which weighed more than 100 lbs., had mauled another biker to death hours before it attacked her. The animal was later tracked and killed by authorities.

You think you know where your life is going. One instant changed everything. Now I feel as though God has given me a mandate to speak to groups, particularly pre-teen girls. There is so much pressure on them to look a certain way. What's important isn't whether you look like a movie star but who you are inside.

I've been biking many times since the attack. Certain things trigger fear, but I'm feeling great emotionally now. I'm just so thankful to be alive. Literally to have been in the jaws of death and live is incredible.

TO CELEBRATE THE END of their first week as ninth graders at William R. Boone High School in Orlando, Fla., Edna Wilks, her friend Amanda Valance and some other students decided to go for a moonlight dip in Little Lake Conway, near Edna's house. "It's very safe," says Edna, then 15, "and we're good swimmers."

But as they splashed in the water the night of Aug. 18, 2001, something grabbed Edna's left arm. "At first I thought it was someone playing around," she says. "Then I saw the alligator's head. I didn't even have time to scream; he just pulled me under. He started spinning me over and over, and I heard something crack in my body. I'm thinking, 'I'm going to die like this.'"

Even as other swimmers headed for the shore and safety, Amanda Valance turned back to try to rescue her good friend. "The alligator was behind us," recalled Valance (right, wading with Edna Wilks in the same lake where their drama unfolded). "I thought, 'I hope God takes us in his hands like I'm taking Edna.'"

For an instant the gator loosened its grip, and Edna burst to the surface and cried for help. "I saw everyone swimming away," she says. "All the boys were heading for shore. I screamed, 'Come back, don't leave me!'"

But everyone did—except for best buddy Amanda, then 14, who churned toward her on a boogie board. "For a second I was like, 'I gotta get out of here,'" says Amanda. "Then I thought, 'No, I can't leave my best friend out here to die.'" When she reached Edna, she saw that the girl's arm was bleeding badly—then, just a few feet away, the gator surfaced and seemed to glare at her. Pushing Edna onto the board, Amanda

The alligator was later captured and killed.

dug into the water and, with her powerful breaststroke, headed toward the shore 50 yards away. The gator began to move, closing in, then submerging. Though petrified, Amanda continued to comfort Edna: "I told her, 'Come on, you can make it.' I was crying."

By the time the two reached shore, Edna's mother, Nancy, was waiting and paramedics were on the way. The gator,

an 11-footer, was later found and shot by wildlife officers. Miraculously, although the reptile had snapped Edna's upper-arm bone and left a foot-long gash, it had missed a major artery. Given another minute, "it would have finished my daughter off," says Nancy, then 42, a homemaker. "Edna would not be alive today if it weren't for Amanda." Adds Edna: "She always said that her biggest fear was being attacked by a shark or alligator, yet she still swam to me."

And Amanda? "I've read about people who were courageous and I always hoped I could be like them," she says. "People come up to me at school and say, 'Gosh, you're the gator girl.' I'm pretty proud of that."

'GATOR GIRL' TO THE RESCUE!

Yanked underwater by an alligator, Edna Wilks learned what it's like to have a really good—and fearless—friend

CRIPPLED JET, MODEST HERO

The hydraulics of his DC-10 blown out, Capt. Al Haynes called on ingenuity and epic calm to save scores of lives

Years later, when Haynes's daughter Laurie Arguello (below) needed a lifesaving operation, Flight 232 passengers raised $500,000. Even after a disaster, a grateful Haynes noted, "something positive can happen."

UNITED FLIGHT 232, WITH 296 PASSENGERS ABOARD, *was cruising uneventfully from Denver to Chicago when Capt. Al Haynes felt the DC-10 shudder. A quick check determined that one of the jet's three engines had exploded. Moments later the plane's hydraulic systems began to fail; shrapnel from the disabled engine, at the rear of the plane, had severed vital hydraulic lines that controlled the wing flaps, elevators, ailerons and rudder. An experienced pilot, Haynes knew that meant he now had only very limited ability to steer the plane or control changes in altitude.*

Using only the throttles of his two remaining engines to control the plane, Haynes, 58, began a slow descent toward the nearest airport in Sioux City, Iowa. Aided by his first and second officers and an off-duty

pilot who was aboard as a passenger, he spiraled the plane down from 37,000 feet in giant right-turning arcs in a desperate attempt to achieve a level approach to the emergency runway.

The following is a distillation of recorded transmissions between the cockpit and the tower during those fateful 41 minutes on July 19, 1989.

CREW: This is United 232. We blew No. 2 engine and we've lost all hydraulics and we are only able to control level flight with asymmetrical [engine thrust] power....

HAYNES: We don't have any controls.

CREW: Don't pull the throttles off.

HAYNES: Start forward.

CREW: Come on, baby, come on, baby....

HAYNES: We're not gonna make the runway, fellas. We're gonna have to ditch this son of a bitch and hope for the best.... Pull back, pull back. Start it down. No, no, no, no, no, not yet. Wait a minute till it levels off.

CREW: We're gonna have to land somewhere out here, probably in a field.

HAYNES: How they doin' on the evacuation?

FLIGHT ATTENDANT: They're put-ting things away, but they're not in any big hurry.

HAYNES: Well, they better hurry. We're gonna have to ditch, I think. ... Sioux City, United 232.

SIOUX GATEWAY CONTROL TOWER: Sioux City.

HAYNES: Sir, we have no hydraulic fluid. I have serious doubts about making the airport. Have you got someplace near we might be able to ditch?

CREW: Gotta put some flaps [down] and see if that'll help.

HAYNES: The hell, let's do it—we can't get any worse than we are—and spin in.

SIOUX CITY: United 232, understand you're gonna try to make it into Sioux City.

CREW: Is this Sioux City down to the right?

HAYNES: That's Sioux City.... See if you can keep us with the throttles in a 10- to 15-degree turn.

CREW: All right, I'll play 'em, I'll play 'em....

OFF-DUTY PILOT: Hi, Al. Denny Fitch.

HAYNES: How do you do, Denny.

FITCH: I'll tell you what. We'll have a beer when this is all done.

HAYNES: Well, I don't drink, but I'll sure as hell have one. . . . We almost have no control of the airplane.... It's gonna be tough ... gonna be rough.

FLIGHT ATTENDANT: So we're gonna evacuate?

CREW: Yeah.

HAYNES: If we can keep the airplane on the ground and stop, standing up, give us a second or two before you evacuate.... "Brace" will be the signal. It'll be over the PA system: "Brace, brace, brace!"

FLIGHT ATTENDANT: And that will be to evacuate?

HAYNES: No, that'll be to brace for the landing. But I really have my doubts you'll see us ... standing up ...

SIOUX CITY: United 232, you're currently 33 miles northeast.

HAYNES: We don't have any brakes.

CREW: No brakes?

HAYNES: Well, we have some brakes....

SIOUX CITY: United 232, your present heading looks good.

HAYNES: We'll see how close we can come to holding it. . . . Right turns are no problem, just left turns.

SIOUX CITY: You're gonna have to widen out just slightly to your left,

"I'm trying to accept that so many were lost," said Haynes shortly after the deadly crash.

> " We have no hydraulic fluid. I have serious doubts about making the airport. Have you got someplace near we might be able to ditch?"

"Al is a reluctant hero," one survivor said of Haynes, who resumed his duties just three months after the accident.

sir, to make the turn to final and also take you away from the city.

HAYNES: Whatever you do, keep us away from the city.

CREW: Keep turning, Al, keep turning right.

HAYNES: You gotta level this sucker off. . . . I want to get as close to the airport as we can. . . .

CREW: We have four minutes to touchdown. . . .

HAYNES: Won't this be a fun landing. . . . Ease it down . . . right there.

CREW: Oh, baby.

HAYNES: We have the runway in sight.

SIOUX CITY: At the end of the runway, it's just wide open field.

CREW: Left throttle, left, left, left, left. . . .

CREW: God!

[*Sound of impact*]

Ten seconds short of touchdown, as passengers braced for an emergency landing, the right wing dipped, caught the ground and sent the plane somersaulting across the asphalt, breaking into large fiery sections and sending parts of the fuselage hurtling into a cornfield. In computer simulations of the same landing, no one had come out alive. But of the 296 persons aboard Flight 232, 184 survived, including the cockpit crew. "There is no hero," Haynes said afterward, "just a group of people, four people, who did their jobs."

Even today, Haynes keeps in touch with a number of the survivors. But foremost in his mind remained those who did not come home. "It's a miracle that 184 lived," he said. "But we cannot forget those people we lost and their families."

The survivors have certainly never forgotten Al Haynes. Fifteen years after the accident, his daughter Laurie Arguello had a rare kind of anemia that required a costly bone marrow transplant that was not covered by insurance. When passengers heard about her plight, they raised more than $500,000 for her treatment. "She went through it beautifully," said Haynes. "I was flabbergasted that they would do that for her, but I'm glad they did."

Haynes was seconds from achieving the impossible by safely landing a DC-10 without using the flaps or rudder.

LOST IN THE DARK

Alone in a pitch-black cave for five days, a father and his sons prayed for a miracle

GARY LUTES'S HEART SKIPPED A BEAT. The acetylene lamp on his son Tim's hard hat should have lasted a good half hour. But after just 10 minutes it began to flicker. The bad news was that Gary, Tim, 9, and Gary's other son, Buddy, 13, were 1,200 feet into a labyrinth of caves in the Smoke Hole recreation area of West Virginia. Worse news, by far, was that Gary had also violated caving's golden rule: *Never* leave your emergency pack behind. Gary's pack, containing water, fuel and a candle, had been snagging on the cave's low ceiling, so he had removed it about 200 feet back. With Tim's light giving way, the trio began crawling and walking back toward where they had left the pack.

Then Tim's lamp went out entirely. Moments later, inexplicably, Buddy's lamp failed too. Crawling and stooping, with only Gary's lamp left, they hurried on. "Dad looked nervous," says Buddy. "I could tell we were lost. He was moving too fast, jerking his head back and forth." Lutes tried to take control of his fear. "I thought to myself, 'I

Gary and his sons Buddy (left) and Tim, revisited New Trout Cave, site of their ordeal.

> " I told the boys, 'There may come a time when one of us is going to go first. If by some chance that happens to be me, I want you to take my shirt [for warmth].' That got them all churned up"

can't let this happen . . . I can't let this happen.'"

Sensing their father's anxiety, the boys began to panic. "Dad, let's get out of here," they pleaded. "We want to get out of here." Then, point-blank, they asked, "Dad, are you lost?" For the first time in Lutes's 20 years of caving, the tunnels seemed terrifyingly unfamiliar. Yet he tried to reassure his sons: "No, I just don't remember these landmarks." He started down a passage, only to turn back. He guessed he had 20 minutes of carbide left.

Then his lamp, too, went out.

Plunged into utter darkness, the three went numb. "Nobody really said much of anything other than the kids asking, 'Are we gonna get out of here? Are we gonna get out of here?'" Lutes recalled later. "I said, 'Yeah, we're gonna get out. I just gotta think.'" For two hours Lutes

weighed the options. He thought of trying to crawl out with the boys clinging to his feet, but "I realized I hadn't even found my way to the pack with a light. How was I going to do it in total darkness?"

Lutes's light had failed in an area of treacherous 6- to 8-ft. drops, so he decided to seek safer ground. Opening the lamps on all three of their hard hats, Lutes gathered enough carbide pellets to ignite one lamp—though he didn't know how long it would last. Then he hustled the boys into a low-ceilinged opening about 50 feet long and 20 to 30 feet wide. In the center there was a large rock on which they could almost stand. They had a moment to scan the room when Lutes's lamp—and the world around them—went black.

Afraid that if they attempted to feel their way to the surface they

would either fall into a pit or just work their way into an even more remote part of the caves, the three huddled together and waited, hoping for help to arrive.

Time, marked by luminous dials, passed with excruciating slowness. "We kept looking at our watches every 10 minutes," says Buddy. Seated side by side on their knee pads to insulate themselves from the cold rock, the three tried to conserve body heat. But soon they were shivering in the damp, 54-degree air. As lunchtime passed, then dinnertime, they talked about the cooler full of cold cuts back in the truck just 60 feet from the mouth of the cave. "By the first night our mouths were feeling dry, like cotton," says Lutes. "I would have given anything for that canteen of water." At about 9:30, bats began making squeaking noises and fluttering around the intruders. "I guess they were checking us out," says Lutes.

Within 24 hours, their growing weakness ended any thought of crawling out. They couldn't stand without becoming dizzy. "Your head would spin like you were on a merry-go-round," says Lutes. He methodically assessed their predicament. The boys' maternal grandparents near Richmond, Va., were expecting them, but not until Thursday night, and other cavers were unlikely to visit New Trout before the weekend. Even if police spotted their truck and sent help, Lutes figured they would be pinned down for at least two days.

By the third day the Luteses were tormented as much by the enclosing darkness as by their hunger. "You couldn't see your hand an inch in front of your face," says Lutes. "Your eyes don't adjust." They dozed off for brief periods, sometimes weeping. Over time, magnesium dioxide dust—from saltpeter mining in the cave more than a century and a half before—filled their mouths and clogged their throats. Lutes and Buddy coughed incessantly, and Tim began retching. "Hundreds of times I told the boys I was sorry," says Lutes. "They kept reassuring me that it wasn't my fault, that they wanted to be there as much as I did."

It was on the third day that Lutes began to think he was dying. He felt a pain in his chest, and he started seeing flashes of light. "I told the boys, 'There may come a time when one of us is going to go first. If by some chance that happens to be me, I want you to take my shirt.' That got them all churned up. I remember the three of us just hugging each other for so long and crying, but I'd gotten dehydrated to

where there were no tears."

Surprisingly, Lutes felt better when he awoke the following morning. But by Friday afternoon he felt himself slipping away again. Lutes imagined he saw a Coke machine, and Buddy hallucinated that he was reclining on their living room La-Z-Boy. That same afternoon Lutes noticed that he and Tim had begun breathing irregularly, an ominous sign. The boys asked what it would be like to die. Their father told them that hypothermia would make them feel warm and fall asleep, while dehydration would make them lose consciousness.

Just as they were giving up hope, Lutes thought he heard someone calling Tim's name. "I thought it was my mind playing tricks on me," he says. "I just lay there and didn't say a thing. It was Tim who sat up and started yelling, and I realized if he was hearing the same thing I was, it must be real."

Fifteen minutes later, their five-day nightmare ended as two rescuers approached. "The lights on their hats seemed like a high beam from a car shining in our eyes," Lutes remembers. "I loved seeing that light."

The rescue efforts had begun two days earlier, when a resident near the cave, noticing that Lutes's truck hadn't been moved for three days, phoned the West Virginia state police, who later contacted the National Speleological Society, which is routinely brought in for cave-rescue assistance.

All three suffered from dehydration, starvation and nerve damage to their feet from lost circulation. Buddy also had a partially collapsed lung, and Tim had to be treated for an infected blister. "It happened; I can't change it now," says Lutes. "But if one of my children had died, I never would have forgiven myself."

"I'm so proud of them," Lutes said of Buddy and Tim (safe and sound back home). "It was by the three of us being together that we made it."

SURVIVING A SHIPWRECK

The *Moorings* went down in minutes; adrift on a raft, three sailors battled hunger, thirst and fear

THE JAMAICA HOSPITAL

Reunited in a hospital after the rescue (from left), Marc Dupavillion, Allison Wilcox and Eddy Provost told what it was like to spend 11 days on a life raft.

THE LIGHTEST OF BREEZES riffled South Carolina's Marsh Harbor Marina on the evening of Friday, Aug. 16, 1991, as the 38-ft. *Moorings* headed out to sea. Crewing the sloop were three experienced sailors: Marc Dupavillion, 26, of Calabash, S.C.; Eddy Provost, 42, of Pawleys Island, S.C.; and Allison Wilcox, 33, of Austin, Texas. The trio had agreed to deliver the new yacht to a Newport, R.I., boat show, a voyage, they thought, that would take no more than five days.

Wilcox, a clinical psychologist, was five months pregnant and saw this as a last great adventure before her marriage in the fall and the birth of her baby. But before casting off, she was troubled by a gloomy premonition. She had heard reports of a tropical depression brewing 500 miles to the south. She was also wary of leaving on a Friday, which in maritime lore can portend bad luck. "I called my fiancé, Steve Voorhies, and I just started crying," Allison remembers.

The first night, seas were calm. By the next day, though, the winds had picked up. "The radio weather report still had the slow-moving storm 450 miles southeast of us," says Eddy, an independent TV producer, "so we weren't worried."

But just past midnight, 60-mph winds drove the waves up to 40 feet high, and Marc was forced to lower the main and try to run with only the foresail and engine. "I heard that the storm was now a hurricane—it was overtaking us," Marc recalls. They were more than 100 miles from shore, and their limited-range, two-way radio wasn't strong enough to call for help. At 2:30 a.m. he stopped the engine, lowered the foresail and, with two sea anchors trailing, set the bow into the wind.

"I thought I'd never see him again," said Wilcox (with then-fiancé Steve Voorhies).

At 6 a.m. Sunday, disaster struck. Winds howled to more than 100 mph, and the waves rose to a mountainous 70 feet. "I was down below listening to the radio, and the others were in their bunks," Marc says. "Then the boat just lifted out of the water and got slammed on its side. We got slammed about five times, and when I went up on deck, you couldn't see because of all the spray. We were on our side, water pouring into the cabin." Clinging to the wildly pitching deck on hands and knees, Marc ordered Eddy and Allison to fill a canvas seabag with food, water and other supplies. In minutes the three had scrambled into the 6-by-8-ft. life raft that Marc had managed to inflate. After the line to the yacht was cut, they watched as the sloop, its mast lights still eerily aglow, slipped beneath the surface.

Immediately afterward, the first of many towering waves crashed down on them, tossing the raft end over end. Lines snapped off the rubber sides, the seabag with their supplies broke free and was lost, and the three tumbled through the orange canopy, tearing it as they flipped upside down. Over the next three hours the raft capsized at least two dozen times. "Imagine a seven-story building falling on you—over and over," says Eddy. At one point, the raft seemed about to sink. Quickly gulping down their only jug of fresh water, they cut the top off the container and used it to bail frantically.

Once, Marc almost drowned when he lost his grip and floated about 100 feet away from the raft. Like the others, he wore a life jacket, but his heavy foul-weather gear weighed him down. As he began to flail his arms, Allison, a strong swimmer, brought him back. "I was history," Marc says. "Then her hand touched mine."

By that afternoon the waves had dropped to 20 feet, the sun was shining, and in the aftermath of the hurricane's passing they took stock of their situation. No food, no fresh water, and Marc hadn't brought his radio-locating beacon because it was broken. Two paddles, three handheld flares, a gallon-size bailer, a sponge and Eddy's sailing knife were all that remained of their supplies. Wet and shivering, they spent the first of many sleepless nights bailing while sitting hip-deep in water.

Before dawn, they unsuccessfully tried signaling a plane with a flare, then used their remaining two flares in a vain attempt to signal the first of two passing ships a half mile away. By Monday morning, Aug. 19, Marc had retreated to a passive state, placing his 6'3" frame in a troughlike space at one end of the raft, while the smaller Allison and Eddy kept it balanced at the other end. "I was totally depressed," says Marc.

Taking charge, Eddy started a routine of bailing water from the raft, having the others strip their clothes off to dry them, swimming next to the raft for brief periods, and devising ways to catch fish. Instead of a 'human being,'" Eddy says, "I became a 'human doing.' I was an Eagle Scout, and I put all those badges to use. I caught our first meal by grabbing a triggerfish with one hand and stabbing it with my knife." From then on, Eddy was the provider. He used the small parachute-shaped sea anchor to catch fish, collected seaweed to eat and harvested barnacles and tiny shrimplike krill from the leaves.

Allison, who had some medical training, became the nurse—though a sometimes overbearing one. "We all had painful saltwater sores and had to dry off." she says. "Every day I'd clean their sores with the sponge. I guess I was like the nurse from hell." She also reminded them that they could exist without water for about a week, so they all agreed not to drink seawater for six days because salt would quicken the dehydration.

During their second afternoon, on Monday, Eddy spotted a pod of about five sperm whales breaching in the distance. As one neared, emerging vertically with its huge head breaking the surface 20 yards away, one eye on the raft, Allison began screaming in fear. But Eddy was enthralled as it swam closer. "I reached out and scratched its head," he says. "It was the natural high of my life."

By the fifth night adrift, they became aware of search planes overhead. Allison, who had the best vision, was the designated lookout and never tired of waving her arms and screaming for help even when it seemed hopeless. "I did a lot of screaming and crying—we all did," she says.

With desperation setting in, they even broached the topic of

whether, in the event of death, their bodies should be thrown into the water or consumed by the survivors. "Toward the end, we were deteriorating fast," Allison recalls. "I thought about ending it while I still had some control over my mind. I thought I would die first, and I was very scared."

By the morning of Aug. 28, the 11th day, the three were severely dehydrated and near death. At 11 a.m. Allison saw the orange stripe of a Coast Guard Hercules cargo plane approach. "I told her to forget it—they'll never see us," Eddy recalls. "But she started waving a paddle anyway." This time the plane dropped smoke bombs to mark the location—some 80 miles off Cape May, N.J.—and a rescue helicopter from the aircraft carrier *America* flew to the site.

Though plagued by nightmares of their ordeal, the three survivors were returned to their homes, weakened but healthy. Happily Wilcox eventually gave birth to a full-term 8½-lb. boy. In the end, "there's nothing courageous in being shipwrecked," says Eddy. "Either you do something to save yourself, or you die. And I just wasn't ready to die."

> " Toward the end, we were deteriorating fast. . . . I thought about ending it while I still had some control over my mind. I thought I would die first"—Wilcox

Abandoning their swamped sailboat amid the fury of Hurricane Bob, the three crew members clung to their raft. Salvation came 11 long days later.

CHAPTER 2

NATURAL DISASTERS

TORNADOES, TIDAL WAVES AND A 100,000,000-VOLT SPEAR

KATRINA STRIKES HOME

The hurricane hit, the levees broke, and New Orleans changed forever

AS EARLY AS FRIDAY, AUG. 26, 2005, Gulf Coast residents began hearing that a major hurricane was headed their way. By the weekend, the mayors of New Orleans and other cities had ordered mandatory evacuations. Many, by choice or because they lacked money, transportation or both, stayed behind. Hurricane Katrina, a Category 4 storm packing 145-mph winds, hit on Monday, Aug. 29, and left more than 1,300 dead, an estimated 1 million displaced and at least $25 billion in damage.

ALICE JACKSON, 52, a part-time reporter for PEOPLE, lives near the coast in Ocean Springs, Miss.: Saturday I evacuated to my friend's house with my 81-year-old mother and my 28-year-old niece. We packed clothes, food, water, axes, a ladder and flares.

On Sunday night, just before the TV went out, a report said, "It's looking better for New Orleans, and the very worst for the Gulfport area." After hearing that, I walked into the other room and said, "I want you to forgive me now, because I think I made a mistake. I'm afraid we're all going to have to fight very hard not to die."

At 1 a.m. winds started pummeling the house. By radio we learned that all three of the emergency operation centers were washed away. Then we lost the radio.

All night I watched a giant pine tree in a neighbor's yard. Suddenly I heard a deafening crack, and I yelled, "Run!" Seconds later the tree smashed through the house. We had escaped to the master-bedroom closet; we covered my mother and niece with a mattress.

Looking outside, we watched the house behind us. The roof would lift, the house would expand, then the roof would fall. Finally the house exploded.

We made it through the night. The next day we tried to check on my house. We were stopped by

"I have nightmares, terrible nightmares," said one Katrina survivor. "But I don't have any more tears to cry." Rescue workers evacuating neighborhoods (left) needed boats to navigate the streets of New Orleans.

debris. Some women were pointing toward an empty slab. They told us, "Last night there was a house there, and a whole family was in it." One of the women screamed, "Where are the children?" We walked toward them, and I stepped on something. It was a little shoe. There with a leg attached, it was a body, buried in mud. I told them as calmly as I could, "Please don't pull this out; let the rescue crews do it."

I arrived at the empty slab of my mother's house first. It had been wiped clean—but miraculously, in the mud, I found her wedding band. The only other thing I found was my dad's paratrooper bracelet from World War II. Those two items are all my mother has left.

My house was completely gone. I knelt down on my slab and said, "I am so grateful that the people I love have lived." And I cried.

BONNIE LAMBERT, 58, Biloxi, Miss.: It started around 5 a.m. My little Pomeranian, Sugar, went into this closet in the center of my house, and I went in there with her. But then the water started sloshing up underneath me and I got up. My refrigerator started floating over to my cooktop. Then the waves came up and my house started floating. I was terrified, and I said, "Okay, if it's my time, let's just get it over with."

But then my deck saved me. It's built around a 650-year-old oak tree, and the tree acted like an anchor. If it weren't for the tree, my house would have floated down the street. All the houses around me are washed away.

GEORGE GRIFFITH, 42, Biloxi, Miss.: I was upstairs watching TV. The wind started howling, so I lay down in the laundry room. Then the water was coming in up to about eight feet. I got in the bathtub upstairs and lay there a few hours, and then the walls were knocked down on three sides of the house. After the walls left, it was time to go. I found an old power line attached to the side of the building and held onto it. The water was over my head and sucking me in and out of the building, beating me back and forth. The water was unbelievably high and loud, like a jet. I was treading water and holding onto the wire for three or four hours. Finally the water went down. Now my house has no walls, no windows. It's just got this big opening where I'm sitting in a recliner.

MICHAEL CLAUDEL, 40, of Waveland, Miss., helped several people and a number of pets flee rising water: We started out in a laundromat, but soon we were standing in three feet of water. We got on top of the dry-

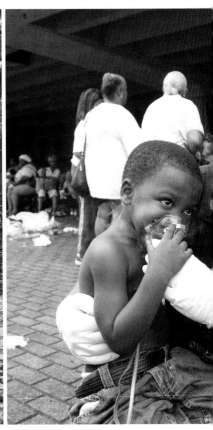

ers, but the water was rushing in. Then we opened up the attic and started putting everybody in there. The water starts coming in, so we busted a hole in the ceiling. We took some boards and put them together so we could cross over the gable of the roof. We walked 40 feet along the back of the roof and we grabbed two 6x12's and laid them across a trailer next to the building, and then we built another bridge to a bathroom on the second floor of another building. The winds were blowing 100, 125 mph easy, but we got everybody over safely, including a blind man, six puppies and three birds.

JAMES OWENS, 35, was in Biloxi, Miss., with his sister, his girlfriend and their five children, ages 3 to 10: We woke up and all of a sudden there was two feet of water. Then it rose to about 5½ feet. I put the children on the top of a closet shelf, and my girlfriend and I stood on top of a TV. We stayed that way for three hours. The kids were crying and screaming, but I was really try-

the house and held on for dear life. I was amazed by the power of the storm. I was getting hit by flying debris, and the rain and wind kept me from breathing right. I felt like I was drowning. And then the eye of the storm passed, and everything got quiet. We lost everything. Katrina didn't care if you were poor or rich; all the houses look the same now. But I'm determined to get my life back.

JAMES GUIDRY, 42, assistant manager for an oil-rig service compa-

stadium lights above the water. I've been through all kinds of storms, but I've never seen such devastation.

TERRIE STEPHENS, 52, volunteered to help at the Mont Belvieu, Texas, shelter: I saw a family with a 16-month-old baby who had just had a liver transplant and was on a feeding tube, and they'd fled the storm. There were so many families who left loved ones who wouldn't leave. One girl told me she was begging family members

Coping (from left): Two men push their truck through floodwaters in New Orleans; a rescuer attends to a child outside the Superdome; a neighbor comforts Sam Miller, 10, whose Pascagoula, Miss., home was destroyed.

ing to stay calm for my kids.

PENNY DEAN, 50, in Pearlington, Miss., survived by climbing onto her roof and hanging on to a tree: When the water started coming in, I grabbed some towels to wipe it up. Then I looked out the window and saw the water rushing at us. When I saw furniture floating by, I thought, "I'm going to die." My husband, Tommy, and I went up to the second floor, but then water started filling up the floor, and we broke out a window and got on the roof. I grabbed on to a tree next to

ny, helicoptered from Port Fourchon to Buras, La., just two hours after Katrina passed: There were houseboats in the middle of the roadway. The major hotel complex was devastated. Suddenly we saw nothing but water and rooftops. Shrimping vessels were beached on the levees. Barges were wrecked. Dead livestock everywhere. I wanted to cry. The only thing you could recognize were the high school

to come. The faces of these people were so stunned. But then to see so much strength and faith and love was humbling. The whole community brought in food, clothing, toys, towels, blankets, and everyone is asking what else can be done. Anyone here on the Gulf Coast knows that the next time it could be our city. We give today, and tomorrow we could be on the receiving end.

WAVE OF DESTRUCTION

Survivors of the 2004 tsunami tell what it's like to be grabbed, churned, spun, held underwater, torn from loved ones—and live

special. I had him late in life, and he's very loving. By about 9 on Sunday morning we got ready to leave. Suddenly a huge wave smashed into our backs. It was like a slap from a giant. I was holding Jothi's hand tightly, but the impact tore us apart and we were lifted into the air. I rolled over and over inside the wave. There were broken bottles, bits of trees—all sorts of debris rolling with me. The next thing I knew I was lying on the beach, aching, scratched all over. I was looking for my son, crying and staggering. Finally I found his body close to the water's edge. His head was buried in the sand. I knew it was him because of his striped blue-and-white T-shirt and his gray trousers. I crouched by his side and wept. Finally some people came and carried his body away.

STEVE MOCKUS, 34, a San Francisco book editor, and **JODY HUMES**, a 31-year-old high school English teacher from San Jose, were reading on the beach at Phi Phi Island, Thailand:

HUMES: The crabs were being weird, running around.

MOCKUS: Maybe they do that every day, but it was new to us. Then I saw Thai people beating like hell back to shore. I saw a low wave come in. Then another came in and knocked us over.

HUMES: I saw a house float away.

MOCKUS: We got blasted from one side of the island to the other. We were in a channel. I was underwater

TRIGGERED BY AN EARTHQUAKE *that erupted on the ocean's floor Dec. 26, 2004, the Indian Ocean tsunami devastated coastal areas in 12 countries and killed more than 230,000 people.*

SUPAT GATEMANEE, 19, was a waiter at a beachfront cafe in Phuket, Thailand, when the sea engulfed him:

It began like an ordinary day. I remember seeing foreigners playing in the sea as I put out tablecloths. Then I went into the kitchen, and when I opened the door to go back out, the water crashed in. As it rose steadily up to my chest, I thought, "I'm dead." I wanted to help my friends, but the water pushed me inland. I remember seeing Tim, our main cook, floating about 16 feet in front of me, then disappearing. I never saw her come up again. Somehow I kept my head above water and was pulled toward the Sheraton hotel terrace, which was on higher ground. I managed to latch onto the terrace railing, and a Thai man who was standing there saw me struggling and pulled me up.

From where I stood, I saw another of our cooks, an elderly lady who was clinging to the trunk of a nearby palm tree, crying. So I waded out, chest deep, and pulled her through the rushing water to safety at the hotel. I thought it was over and returned to the terrace. But a second wave hit. This one was about twice as high, more than seven feet, and it tossed me back into the water. I grabbed onto a floating piece of a thatch roof but was forced to let go. Luckily, the water pulled me back to the hotel, and another man helped me out.

Later I found my boss and some other employees. The restaurant had been bamboo with a thatch roof. In a blink the second wave tore it apart. We rode to my boss's house. No one spoke, no one cried. I was in shock. The next morning, I went back to help look for the dead. We found Tim's swollen body in a canal. We were good friends. She has two daughters.

It was good luck that saved me. I really enjoyed Phuket. It was my first time living by the sea. It was beautiful, and it was big. Now I'm never going back.

SELVI, 50, a fisherman's wife and mother of four, was gutting fish on the beach near her small village near Chennai, India:

During school holidays, my youngest son, Jothi, who's 9, comes to the beach with me. He is very standing up. But Jody and I were separated. I found a plastic kayak and grabbed it. A young Thai girl climbed in. She had what looked like a roofing nail sticking in her neck. She seemed to be doing well for someone with a nail in her neck. I yelled for help and saw a tour boat. We managed to get in.

HUMES: I think I was hit with an air conditioner. I was coughing gasoline, and my bikini came completely off. I was underwater clawing debris. Finally I found a roof to hold onto, but it disintegrated, and I was holding onto a piece of wood. I found a Frenchwoman in the water, and we saw another boat. We reached it, and a naked Thai man held out his hand. The naked man found a T-shirt and tore it in two to share with me. There was a little French boy screaming for his mother. And an Asian woman who had nearly lost her arm, and people were trying to hold it onto her. We moved onto a ferry boat, then a larger tour boat. A man gave me a Coke, and I vomited dirt, gasoline and little bits of nature. Then, sometime around 4 or 5 p.m., I looked out and saw Steve on the deck of another boat. When I got to Phuket, I saw the Asian woman covered up. She didn't make it.

DWAYNE MEADOWS, 38, a Honolulu marine biologist, was on vacation in Khao Lak, Thailand. He was in his bungalow when the wave hit:

I heard the classic train-rumbling noise. Then I saw the wave. It wasn't large, but I knew what it was. It came in about 30 feet high and went over the bungalow. The walls started collapsing. I snuck out the side, but was submerged and churning. I can hold my breath two or three minutes, but I was panicking. After a minute or so, I really thought it was the end. I was spinning, being smashed into things. At the end of my capacity, I suddenly came up for air. When the lower half of a mannequin swam by, I held onto it. Two women, a Thai and a German, were trapped in a mass of floating debris.

I was hyperventilating and tired, but I got to the Thai woman, who kept saying she couldn't swim. I gave her the mannequin and said I'd help her to the shore. But she freaked out and held onto a piece of roof she'd been clinging to. I had to leave her. The German woman floated off. I started swimming to shore and reached the beach.

When the monster wave swept through the grounds of the Holiday Inn Resort near Phuket, Australian tourist Jillian Searle was poolside with sons Lachie, 5, and Blake, 2. The water, which quickly surged up to Searle's neck, was too powerful for her to hold onto both boys without all three of them drowning. "I could feel him squeezing me," Searle said of her older son, who could not swim. "And he said to me, 'Don't let go of me, Mummy.' "

Hoping to save at least one of her children and thinking that the older one had a better chance at survival, Searle tore Lachie's hand from hers, pleading, "Someone take my son!"

Nearby, Alyce Morgan, 17, was fighting for her own life. But the Australian teenager, on vacation with her family, grabbed Lachie and struggled onto the top of a bar counter, trying desperately to keep his head above water. When Morgan felt herself being pulled under, she, too, let him go. Witnessing the entire scene from a second-floor hotel balcony, Searle's husband, Bradley, rushed downstairs to help—but was blocked by a wall of water. When it finally receded, he found Jillian and Blake hanging onto beach furniture near the pool. Together, they frantically searched the devastated area for Lachie, fearing the worst. "There is no way I can live my life knowing that I took his hand off mine," Jillian told her husband.

Hours later, they rejoiced when they discovered he had survived. Tossed along by the current, Lachie had grabbed onto a still-standing lobby door. After clinging to it for two hours, he was discovered by a security guard and carried to safety. Reunited with him and back in their home city of Perth, the Searles are counting their blessings—and keeping both boys close. Said Bradley: "You never want to let them out of your sight."

ONE MAN TAKES IN 230 REFUGEES

After watching the deluge destroy his village of Lampaseh, Indonesia, Aminullah Usman, a 47-year-old banker, reached out to help others, opening the doors of his home to survivors. "I told them all, 'You are my family now. This is your home. Stay as long as you like.' " Within two days he had taken in 230 people. "I have nowhere to go," said a survivor who lost her parents, three sisters and only child. "Mr. Usman is a good man with a big heart."

TAKEN BY A TORNADO

Torn from her mother's arms by a whirlwind, tiny Aleah Crago survived

MAY 3 1999

AFTER A SUCCESSION OF TORNADOES *carved an 80-mile path of devastation across central Oklahoma on May 3, 1999, taking 41 lives and reducing nearly 1,500 buildings to rubble, one unforgettable image gripped the nation: a mud-covered 10-month-old baby named Aleah Crago cradled against the chest of her rescuer, Grady County deputy sheriff Robert Jolley. Jolley, then 27, and Aleah's mother, Amy, 19, told* PEOPLE *how Aleah survived the twister that roared through the community of Bridge Creek, where 11 people, including Amy's mother, were killed.*

AMY CRAGO: Looking out the window of my family's house at around 4:30 as we listened to TV weather reports, we [Amy; Aleah's father, Ben Crosby, then 20; and Amy's parents, Robert Williams, 47, and Catherine Crago, 44] could only see a big black storm cloud. Then we saw the big white cloud circulating around it and knew that was the tornado. There was no time to react, no place to go. We all huddled in the hall closet. Everybody was sort of holding on to Aleah, but she was sitting in my lap. As the storm got closer, it was very, very loud, more like a jet than a train. It has its own smell—you know how plywood smells when it's freshly cut?

Then it ripped the roof off the house and sucked Ben and the baby and me up and out. I can't pinpoint when I let go of her. I just had her, and then I didn't. It was really bright, and the debris was hitting us. It blew me up and I hit a tree. That's the last time I remember holding her. After that I was just fighting it and trying to keep it from taking me wherever it was taking me. I didn't know where, but I knew I didn't want to go.

Finally, I put my head down and put my hands over my head, like they teach you in school. From that point on, all I could think was, I'm gonna die. And then the storm was gone. When I looked up, I was about 100 feet from where the house had been.

My house was gone. The house across the street was gone. It looked like somebody had dropped a bomb. I began looking for everybody, but I couldn't find anybody.

ROBERT JOLLEY: Anticipating a lot of damage, I followed the tornado about 20 miles as I patrolled the southeast corner of the county. I turned onto a gravel road in Bridge Creek and thought, Huh, there are supposed to be houses here. But there weren't any. I saw a man [Robert Williams] staggering, disoriented. I asked if anyone else was around. He said, "No, they're all dead." He was calling for Amy, but I couldn't get him to tell me who she was or how old. So I'm looking for someone named Amy. I found her mother, Catherine Crago, first, pinned facedown, half of her body beneath a flatbed trailer that had been thrown by the incredible winds.

I knew that if anybody was left alive, they'd be in the tree line, about 100 feet east of the destroyed house's foundation. That's where all the debris was. I was scanning that area on foot when I saw movement. I didn't know what it was, it was so small, so slight. I walked over and reached into a mound of chicken wire, paper and other debris, and I grabbed her leg. It was warm. I said to myself, Hey, this isn't a doll. I remember thinking how much she looked like my 18-month-old daughter.

When I rubbed the mud from her ears and eyes, only then did she start to cry. I found a shirt to wrap her in; then I drove one-handed to a triage center, holding her face against my chest to keep her warm. I kept telling her, "Come on, keep crying for me."

AMY CRAGO: The whole three or four hours after I was driven by paramedics to the hospital, I thought Aleah was dead. The only thing I could picture was three big coffins—for my mother, father and Ben—and one little one. Finally, the nurses came and asked me if I had a 10-month-old baby. [Aleah escaped with a bruised lung and a deep scratch on her left thigh. Amy was treated for head injuries. Williams suffered a chipped collarbone. The baby's father, Crosby, who was blown 150 feet through the air, sustained multiple injuries.]

I thank God every day Aleah is still here with me. I'm not really religious—I haven't been to church since I was 14—but I'm gonna go back tomorrow.

Pulled from a pile of debris by Robert Jolley (above, in the picture that made newspapers nationwide), Aleah Crago was reunited with mom Amy (left, in 1999).

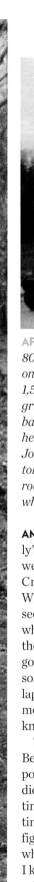

TRAPPED IN A BLIZZARD

Marooned for nine days in a winter storm, Jim Stolpa left his wife and baby in a tiny cave, hiked through snowdrifts and guided rescuers back in time

THREE DAYS AFTER CHRISTMAS, 1992, the Stolpa family—Jim, his wife, Jennifer, and their baby Clayton—piled into their pickup to begin the long trek from their home in Paso Robles, Calif., to Pocatello, Idaho, where they were to attend a funeral for Jim's maternal grandmother. Jim, 21, a satellite-equipment repairman, figured they would need a couple of days to make the 1,000-mile trip, and, as planned, they stopped that first night at his mother's house in Castro Valley, outside Oakland.

Jim's mother, Muriel Mulligan, who had already gone on to Idaho, phoned and urged him to postpone the drive because a snowstorm was battering Northern California and several roads were closed. "Don't

do it. Don't drive in this weather," she pleaded. "I don't want to go to three more funerals."

Ignoring her advice, Jim and his family set off the next morning. Interstate 80, the route they had planned to take northeast, was closed. So the couple bought maps at a gas station and plotted a course on smaller roads. Jennifer, 21, who had been in the Army Reserve until shortly after her marriage in April 1991, served as navigator.

Late that night the Stolpas passed the one-house town of Vya, Nev. (pop. 2), near the California border. Trying to hook up with State Route 140, they continued east on County Road 8A, a two-lane dirt road that was choked with snow. The farther they drove, the

deeper it got. Soon they were stuck.

In the morning the couple tried digging out the truck, but it proved impossible. All they could do was wait for help. For three days and four nights, as snow continued to fall, they stayed as upbeat as possible. "I told myself," said Jennifer, "'If you can make it through basic training, you can make it through this.'" They nibbled on corn chips, cookies, Jennifer's prenatal vitamins and fruitcake. Periodically, they started the truck to turn on the heat and listen to the radio.

When the Stolpas failed to show up for the funeral, Jim's stepfather, Kevin Mulligan, a media consultant, alerted radio and TV stations and newspapers about the missing family and pressed authorities to find them. But no one knew which route they had taken.

When Saturday, Jan. 2, broke clear and bright, "we had to decide whether to stay put and die or do something," Jim said. They decided to walk northeast toward Route 140, which they figured would be about 20 miles. In the truck the pair left a note written on what had been Jennifer's Christmas list. "If we are already dead don't mind the rest of this letter," Jim wrote. "But if we are nowhere to be found, we have started walking to 140." Jennifer added, "We are carrying with us a 5 mos. old baby. HELP!!!"

Then the couple pulled on almost every item of clothing they had: gloves, panty hose, three pairs of sweatpants, four sweatshirts and two long winter jackets each. They slid plastic garbage bags between layers of socks. They bundled up Clayton inside two sleeping bags and stuffed him into a maroon gar-

"Jennifer is just as much of a hero," said husband Stolpa (opposite, with his wife and their child Clayton). With Stolpa's guidance, Dusty Ferguson found mother and child safe and protected in a small cave (left).

ment bag, along with the little food they had left. Jim tied the bag to his belt and towed it through the snow like a sled. To help herself, Jennifer recited cadences from basic training or repeated the mantra of *The Little Engine That Could*: "I think I can, I think I can. . . ."

Late Sunday morning they stood on a hill and searched the horizon for Route 140. It was nowhere in sight. "Oh my God," Jennifer exclaimed. "We're not going to make it!" In desperation they decided to hike back to the truck. But as the day wore on, the temperature dropped and the wind began to howl. Following an old cattle trail, they found a small canyon and spent the night huddled in a sheltered outcropping.

By morning it was snowing again. "There's no way I'm going to be able to walk today," Jennifer told Jim. "I'm going to try to find a cave where we can stay." Moments later she found a tiny indentation barely big enough to crawl into. Jennifer squeezed inside. Jim handed her the sleeping bags and Clayton and wedged the garment bag over the entrance to block the wind. Then he told her he was going for help.

"Saying goodbye to him was the scariest thing in the whole world," Jennifer remembered.

Jim walked the 14 miles back to the truck that night. By 7:30 the next morning, Tuesday, he set out on foot, pushing through an endless sea of white snow. Whenever he felt hungry, he would shove snow into his mouth, and every so often, when he just couldn't make his frozen feet go another step, he would flop down onto some sagebrush for a catnap. Late Wednesday morning Jim spotted something. "I started screaming at the top of my lungs and jumping up and down," he says.

"Jesus Christ!" thought David Peterson, driving his truck down the road. "There's a cow wandering out there!" When Peterson, Washoe County's road supervisor, pulled closer, he saw a man who was shuffling, his "feet frozen up into big balls." Frantically, Jim told Peterson about his stranded wife and baby. "I thought he must have been a little delirious," admitted Peterson, 52, who hadn't heard about a lost family. "He was just out there too many days. Nobody could survive that long."

But back home in Vya, Peterson checked out Jim's story. It was all too true, and Peterson immediately began to organize a rescue effort. Jim begged to go along but was in no condition to do so. Over and over he told Peterson to look for the blue sweatshirt he had tied to a bush in front of the cave.

Peterson and Dusty Ferguson, a heavy-equipment operator, took off in Peterson's truck. For five hours they followed the path blazed by a snowplow. Somewhere behind them, more than two dozen paramedics, deputies and even a dog rescue team fanned out, looking for signs of Jennifer and Clayton. When snow began to fall, rescuers began to lose hope. "With the storm coming and the darkness, I knew it was now or never," Peterson said. Just then his radio crackled to life: The snowplow driver had spotted the blue sweatshirt.

The baby came through the ordeal unscathed, but doctors amputated parts of Jim's and Jennifer's frostbitten feet. Still, they knew they were fortunate to be around at all. And Jim was determined to avoid ever making the same mistake: "Never again will I not listen to my mother."

STRUCK BY LIGHTNING

The odds of being hit by lightning in your lifetime are less than 1 in 600,000. Sherri Spain knows what it's like to be the 1

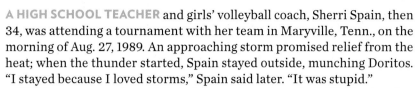

A HIGH SCHOOL TEACHER and girls' volleyball coach, Sherri Spain, then 34, was attending a tournament with her team in Maryville, Tenn., on the morning of Aug. 27, 1989. An approaching storm promised relief from the heat; when the thunder started, Spain stayed outside, munching Doritos. "I stayed because I loved storms," Spain said later. "It was stupid."

Within moments, she said, "a jerk went through my body." Lightning that struck a steel door behind her had entered the back of her skull and exited through her right heel. "I was lifted, the Doritos exploded."

Student Dawn Platt, then 16, saw her coach fall to the ground in convulsions. "I held her hand and called her name, but she didn't respond," said Platt. "I thought she was dead. All I could do was scream for help and pray."

Spain was alive, but seriously injured. She lost the sight in her right eye and most of the hearing in her right ear; she also suffered erratic brain function, heart arrhythmia and severe muscle weakness on her right side. Eerily, her dark brown hair, drained of pigment, turned blonde. "She looked like she'd had a stroke—her arm was curled up, mouth drooping, and she couldn't walk," recalled her husband, Robert. But Spain's gravest traumas weren't visible. A history and geography teacher, she had incurred memory loss so catastrophic she could no longer identify letters and numerals, much less read or write. In almost constant pain and plagued by depression and insomnia, Spain underwent extensive psychotherapy and had to relearn basic intellectual skills ("I practiced every day until I was able to build a new memory," she said) before returning to the classroom in January 1990. "I had no memory at all for historical facts," she said. While teaching remained a struggle, Spain tried to come to grips with her enduring fears by returning to the spot in Maryville where lightning had altered her life. "I stood there for the longest time in front of the gym—I could smell the rain from the time of the accident," she said. "I broke down and cried the rest of the day." Nature, of course, offers other reminders, particularly during the dog days of summer. "My heart [still] races during a storm," she said. "I have to see it—I feel I can control it if I know where it is. But I want Robert holding me."

Though grateful her mom had been spared, daughter Stevie, then 6, was shocked when Spain (in 1997) came home from the hospital. "She didn't look like my mother," she said.

CHAPTER 3

CRASHES, SHIPWRECKS & REALLY BAD LUCK

REMINDER: BE GRATEFUL WHEN TRANSPORTATION WORKS

'WE'RE GOING TO CRASH'

As the pilot guided Flight 1420 through a vicious thunderstorm toward the airport, Randy Hill had a very bad feeling

ARKADELPHIA, ARK., *attorney Randy Hill was eager to get home from Phoenix, where he and two colleagues had taken a lengthy deposition on June 1, 1999. The first leg of his trip was just fine. But when he landed in Dallas to catch American Airlines Flight 1420, his connecting flight to Little Rock, Hill, 39, learned that it was being delayed by bad weather in Arkansas. The announced half-hour delay turned into an hour, then two, before the plane, with 139 passengers and six crew members aboard, taxied onto the runway.*

I called my wife, Jessica, and said, "By the time I get home, it'll be 1 a.m. Don't wait up." Then I phoned a colleague to tell him how the deposition went. He said, "Man, they just issued tornado warnings up here. The weather is terrible." But I wasn't concerned. I assumed that by the time we got to Little Rock either the storms would have passed or we'd circle until we could land safely.

We boarded at 10:20. I was in coach seat 12F by the window—the last seat before the wing, probably 10 rows from the nearest exit. My two lawyer friends sat separately—Brian Boyce was two rows behind me, and Clark Bruster in the back. All I had with me was an overnight bag, my briefcase, cell phone and pager. I also had a little framed picture of Jessica I always carry.

When we took off, the pilot cheerfully announced, "Out the left window there will be a light show tonight"—meaning lightning. Still, the flight was smooth until the end. I was thumbing through a magazine when the pilot said, "We'll be landing in 10 minutes. We're going to have to go around and come in from the north."

It was a little bumpy as we started our descent, but when we made our approach you could see a horrible storm off to the west. Eerily, every time the lightning flashed it illuminated what appeared to be a black wall. That was the hail and rain moving toward us. The pilot made one pass at the airstrip but decided not to land. It was now raining so hard it looked like solid water out the window. Most people were still reading, but I was agitated. I looked at the concerned lady in the aisle seat and said, "We're going to

crash if he tries to land this thing."

Just as the storm was seemingly the worst, he took us in. As we were coming down, rocking all over, he was gunning it, then backing off; you could hear the engine whine and shudder. Somebody said the stewardess told them to brace themselves. Then we hit the runway real hard, and I knew we were in bad trouble. We bounced from side to side, tilted and skidded, and people started screaming.

In the 10 seconds or so that passed from the time we hit the ground until we crashed, I had three distinct thoughts: The first was that I was mad at whoever made the horribly stupid decision to land, the second was that I was so grateful Jessica [who was expecting their first baby] wasn't on that plane, and the third was a sadness that I wasn't going to see my baby.

When we passed the last light on the runway we were still going very fast, and I thought, "It's over. We're heading right for the river." We broke through the approach lights, through the fence and did a 180, like one of those whip things in a carnival. Then we just

"Everything was orange with fire," a passenger recalled after Flight 1420 (left) crashed and broke into sections. Randy Hill (right, with his wife, Jessica) was later credited with keeping his cool and guiding others to safety. "There was a lot of bravery," said Hill. "I was glad to help, but I wouldn't give credit to anyone but God."

stopped. At first there was complete silence. Then people started screaming, "Get out! Get out! It's on fire!"

I was evidently sitting over one of the gas tanks and got drenched with nauseating-smelling jet fuel. I was a long way from an exit, but the plane had fractured right at my seat. There was a crack, but I still had to break through a lot of insulation and paneling. That's how I got my hands cut up, because it was shredded aluminum, and Lord knows what else. Somehow I forced about a 10-inch opening. Ahead of me were a jumble of broken seats and what looked like bodies. Behind me I could see the fire coming, and here I'm covered in jet fuel.

So that little hole was my only way out. I turned sideways and tried to ease through, and just as I get about halfway to freedom, my pants get caught. I'm now hanging halfway out of the plane—legs inside, upper body outside, with the ground maybe six feet below. By then other people had seen that I'd created a new exit. They're screaming, "Get out! Get out!" But I'm

jammed in, and they're pushing on me, trying to crawl over me. I kick my feet furiously and know that the flames are just a few feet away. I'm a hot dog about to be cooked.

Then my pants rip, and I fall head-first into some mud. Two girls who'd been sitting a row or two behind me followed me out. I vaguely remember breaking their fall. In fact, several people fell on me—they were pouring out.

Then I started running as fast as I could, expecting the aircraft to explode. It was hailing fiercely, and the wind had to be blowing 60 to 80 mph. With the lightning flashes I noticed some big round bales of hay. I ran over to three elderly people who were standing around in shock. "Come with me," I said. "We've got to get behind this bale or we're going to be hit by lightning." One bolt struck so close it seemed to knock one of the ladies down. She's standing beside me, then "Boom!"— white light everywhere, and she's on the ground.

Finally, after about a half hour, the storm moved away. I peered over the hay at the plane and saw the flames were getting bigger. I knew Clark was sitting near the tail, and I could see that section burning. A while later I saw Brian, and we both felt helpless.

By then the water was ankle-deep, and it was freezing. Spread out around us were people with cuts and broken limbs. My hands, arms, legs and head were cut, and I was having trouble

breathing. After the first fire trucks finally arrived, I flagged one down and got in back along with a lady who had a bad gash on her leg and a badly burned little girl.

A school bus took us to a hangar where a triage area had been set up. I called Jess. "Hon," I said, "the plane crashed. I'm hurt, but I'll be okay." I had to wait until 3 a.m. before a bus arrived and took me to Southwest Regional Medical Center. I got off the bus, and a guy in scrubs lit up a cigarette! I yelled, "Could you please put that out? I'm covered with jet fuel!"

Just after 3, I called Jess again on somebody's cell phone and told her she could come pick me up. It goes without saying that we were very happy to see each other. When I woke up early in the morning, Jess said, "You know, today's our anniversary." I just started crying. I hugged her and said, "Well, I didn't have a chance to get you anything." And she said, "I've got the best gift I can have. I've got you back."

Of the passengers and crew, 11 died, including the pilot, and at least 88 were injured. Hill suffered a partially collapsed lung, fractured ribs and contusions; both of his legal partners survived. The subsequent investigation determined that the crew, admittedly fatigued, made mistakes that led to the crash. The airline later settled a number of related lawsuits.

THE WRONG RUNWAY

John Diaz lived through the Singapore Airlines crash with memories he'd rather forget

HAVING GROWN UP *in New Orleans, John Diaz had seen his share of hurricanes. He didn't like what he saw when he arrived at the Chiang Kai-shek Airport for his Oct. 31, 2000, flight from Taipei to Los Angeles. Winds whipped across the tarmac, and sheets of water poured down from the sky. Still, when the announcement came to board Singapore Airlines' Flight SQ006, Diaz, 50, a resident of Santa Monica, Calif., and an executive with MP3.com, assumed that the airline knew what it was doing and would clear the Boeing 747-400 for takeoff only if conditions were safe.*

I remember getting on and feeling the jumbo jet shaking from the wind. I got on last, and I got into the farthest front seat in first class. I just glued myself to that window, watching everything, like when we were kids in New Orleans watching the sky for a storm.

I've never seen a plane move so fast to get out to the runway. I sat down, and we immediately taxied out. I could feel us lifting off, and then just seconds later I felt a terrible jolt, followed by a second smaller jolt. I've been in motorcycle accidents, and I've never felt anything like this. Strange, but I didn't feel surprised or shocked. I didn't feel afraid particularly. You know what I thought? I felt validated. I thought, "See, I told them so. We shouldn't have taken off, and now they've killed me."

As the jet began to rise, it struck some construction equipment that had been left on the runway. Then it collided with a concrete barrier and split into three sections.

That's when the fire started, and I could see flames coming up around me, and the cabin began to fill with smoke. At that point I jumped into the aisle and I took a couple of steps. Then I reached back for my bag. When I turned, I couldn't see where I'd come from because it was engulfed in flames. I ran down the aisle toward the emergency door.

While I was going to the door, I remember a video screen melting in

"I don't know why I got out and someone else didn't," said Diaz. The 747-400 struck equipment (top) on a runway not in use.

front of me. It was like someone had taken a blowtorch to a wax figure. I thought, "Why aren't I melting if metal is melting?" It didn't feel like slow motion. I felt very focused and clear. I remember noticing the expression on the faces of some of the dead. I remember one guy's face—he was lying there dead and he looked stunned. And then I saw other people just sitting in their

seats dead, and they were on fire. I think that some passengers froze. I was told by some survivors that flight attendants put damp cloths over their mouths, which saved them from the scorched, damaged lungs that I have.

For a while I thought that very few of us—up front in first—were the only survivors. I think the people in business and in the first rows of coach had very little chance. From what I saw, they were all dead. I understand that the fuel tanks were right underneath them. Where I was, everything was dark and full of smoke from the jet fuel. I think I saw the ground at one point. It was as if the plane was disintegrating under my feet.

You cannot imagine the heat in that cabin. It was like a coffin on fire. I can't talk about some of the things I saw. Later I saw a woman flatline in a triage room at the airport. She died right in front of me, but that was nothing compared to what I saw in that plane. It was

Dante's *Inferno*. If any of the jet fuel got on you, you would burn.

Then I saw other passengers at the emergency door. A couple of people were trying to get it open. I slammed my weight against it, and it popped open. It was then that I felt a rebirth. I had known I was going to die—I was sure of it—until that door popped open. Then I thought there was hope. Some others went out first, and I followed them. I got tangled up in the escape chute. I felt like a turkey in a plastic bag, but I fought my way free, and then we all ran like hell. I didn't see it, but I could feel the explosion behind me.

I'm not sure why I reacted the way I did—to be so calm and focused. Maybe it has something to do with my everyday discipline. I lift weights two hours a day, six days a week. Maybe that's it. I think, though, that I was just lucky: I was sitting in the right seat; I didn't get splashed with jet fuel; I was near a door. I grew up Catholic, and I do have my own private spirituality,

but I'm not sure, really, exactly what to think of this. I can tell you that this is all beyond wonderful, and I am very grateful.

Eighty-two of the 179 passengers on board died. A subsequent investigation determined that by the time the pilot realized he was on the wrong runway, the jet was going too fast to stop; the airline later accepted responsibility and offered compensation to victims' families. The impact was enough to compress every joint in Diaz's body, bruising him from head to foot, and his lungs were scorched by the toxic smoke from burning jet fuel. But he suffered more than physical injuries.

I know I'm going to need some help with this, and I've already made an appointment with a therapist. Right now all these emotions are just rolling through me. Anger and despair and depression and incredible gratitude and sorrow—terrible sorrow for those dead. I don't know what the result of this will be for me. But I will be changed.

THE SHIP GOES DOWN

The *Express Samina* sank in minutes, and U.S. tourists Heidi Hart and Christine Shannon scrambled for their lives

IT WAS ABOUT 5 P.M. *Sept. 26, 2000, when the ferry* Express Samina *cast off from Piraeus, the port city of Athens, bound for the Aegean island of Paros. Among the more than 540 passengers and crew were two friends from Seattle, Heidi Hart, 26, an accountant, and Christine Shannon, 32, a preschool teacher. An hour out, the wind came up and the temperature dropped rapidly.*

Five hours into their voyage, the 345-ft. ferry's engines surged. Hart and Shannon assumed they must be nearing their destination. Instead the frantic crew were trying to steer clear of a rocky islet two miles off Paros. Despite the fact that a lighthouse atop the rock was visible from several miles around, the ferry, inexplicably, was headed straight for it.

HART: I felt us hit the rock and looked up, and the rock was straight in front of me, lit up. It looked like a movie set. It was like, "This isn't real, they're playing a joke on us. This must be a big Styrofoam rock next to the dock."

SHANNON: We looked at each other and laughed and kind of went, "What's that?"

HART: You could hear it tear the side of the boat. I looked at Christine and said, "We're going down. We have to get off the boat now."

The collision knocked out the lights and touched off a panic. Adding to the confusion, the crew issued no instructions. Shannon and Hart noticed that many of the life jackets appeared ancient. With few of the 63-man crew in sight, passengers were forced to lower the lifeboats themselves.

HART: We knew we were going to fend for ourselves. Everybody started running toward the back of the boat, and the back was the part that was sinking. So we started to run to high ground. I got pushed by a couple of men running past me and hit my head on the railing.

SHANNON: That was the first right decision: We went where nobody was.

HART: The boat was tilting so much that we were holding on to the guardrails so we wouldn't slide down to the side that was sinking.

SHANNON: I looked over Heidi's shoulder and saw somebody motioning to me. I said, "Go!" and I grabbed her and we just went. A man was at the top of some metal stairs leading down to the next floor, where there was a lifeboat with several people already on board.

SHANNON: When the boat hit the water, there were waves, and we almost capsized. Then we were smashed against the bottom of the ferry.

HART: We were piled on top of each other. It wasn't like everybody was sitting in their seats.

Finally the group maneuvered the lifeboat clear of the ferry. Over the wind and waves, Shannon and Hart could hear people shouting in the water, but they had trouble seeing them. They managed to rescue two men. Just when things seemed to stabilize, Hart noticed the lifeboat was leaking.

SHANNON: Heidi told me, "We're taking on water." There's a hole in the boat, and I lean back and tell the guy behind me. He looks at me and he says, "Yes, we're going down." The waves were just huge. Water was hitting us in the face, and that added to the confusion.

It took the Express Samina *only 38 minutes to sink, but not before the captain had gotten off a distress signal. Several British warships in the vicinity rushed to the scene, along with Greek Coast Guard vessels. A flotilla of local boats from Paros responded as well, their crews risking their lives in the punishing swells.*

Forty minutes after the sinking, a pair of trawlers guided Hart and Shannon's lifeboat to shore, where they were taken to a clinic. Not until the next morning, while watching coverage on television, did they realize the extent of the tragedy. Searchers recovered the bodies of 80 victims, including a 16-month-old boy. For days, neither woman could stop crying. It was the worst Greek maritime disaster in more than 30 years.

HART: It's so scary to think of how close we were.

SHANNON: Those people on the island were just so good to us. They lost a lot of loved ones, but they were so good to us.

As the *Express Samina* (below) sank, passengers escaped in rafts (bottom, left) and lifeboats. "I'm pretty proud of us, actually," said Hart (bottom, right, in jeans, with Shannon back at their Athens hotel). The pair helped save two men.

DRIFTING AWAY

As searchers give up hope, two teens are found alive after a week at sea

ON SUNDAY MORNING, April 24, 2005, Troy Driscoll, 15, and his best friend, Josh Long, 17, were looking forward to a leisurely day of fishing. The high school students from North Charleston, S.C., hadn't been out more than 20 minutes when a vicious riptide grabbed hold of their 15-ft. boat.

Josh: We tried to put the anchor down, but it wouldn't catch. We just drifted farther and farther away. Hours went by. We tried to wave people down, but nobody saw us. The last thing I saw was the towers on shore that lead cargo ships in. By dark we couldn't see a thing. The next morning there was no land in sight. All we could do was pray.

The night before, when the boys— who had no cell phone or emergency equipment—hadn't returned, their frantic parents called the Coast Guard.

Eddie Long, Josh's father: It was the hardest night of my life, walking that beach, knowing that my son and Troy were out there somewhere. It was cold, and the waves picked up.

Josh: We were soaking wet, clinging to each other, trying to keep warm. We'd doze off, but the waves kept crashing into the boat, washing over us, so we couldn't ever get to sleep.

Troy: During the next day, it got so hot we took a couple of dips to cool off. But then the sharks came around, and we just didn't go into the water anymore.

Josh: Far from shore, the water turns clear, like blue Gatorade. Troy begged me, "Please, let me drink just a little." I said, "If you drink it, you'll die." Then [one day] it began to drizzle. I had my mouth wide open to catch drops, but it didn't rain hard enough. I started licking the water from the deck.

Troy: Josh woke up screaming that we were at the store and had to buy some Mountain Dew. I was like, "Bro, we're out in the middle of the water, and there's no Mountain Dew." I was so hungry I ate a jellyfish and waited overnight to see if it would kill me. It didn't. They're slimy, gushy things, but I ate about 100 of them.

Josh: Troy was so hungry he wanted to cut off a finger and eat it. At one point he said, "Please help me get out of here or kill me." I said, "I can't do that."

The Coast Guard used boats, helicopters and airplanes in an exhaustive search. But by sunset on Tuesday, April 26, after 2½ days had passed with no sign of the boys, the Coast Guard rescue mission became a recovery operation.

Eddie Long: They told us that in a week to 10 days the bodies would

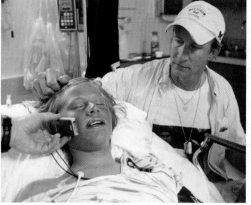

Families reunited (left): Josh (in black) with his parents, Connie and Eddie, and Troy with his parents, Deb Fowler and Tony Driscoll. At sea in their small boat (above, right), said Driscoll (above, left, with his dad), "I dreamt about strawberry milk and ice cream."

By Saturday, April 30, seven days after they set out, the boys were drifting seven miles off Cape Fear and 111 miles from where they had launched.
Josh: Something about Saturday morning was different. When the sun came up, it was a beautiful color. I saw a rainbow off to the left, and there were dolphins playing all around the boat.

Finally, later that day, two fishermen spotted something in the distance.
Ben Degutis, 70: At first I didn't know what it was. As we got closer I could see people waving, and holy mackerel, it was two young guys in this tiny boat. One was yelling, "Thank God!"
Eddie Long: I was outside and heard

a commotion. They gave me the phone, and Josh said, "I miss you, Daddy."
Tony Driscoll, Troy's dad: When I finally saw Troy, it was like him being born all over again. The joy in my heart was that huge.

During their ordeal Long lost 30 lbs. Driscoll was hospitalized for three days for second-degree burns on his face and feet.
Troy: I'll go out again fishing, for sure—in a boat with two motors.
Josh: While we were out there, we dreamed about the biggest sundae you could imagine—the ultimate sundae. Troy and I are going to meet at an ice cream place and have that sundae.

become gaseous and rise to the surface. I went out on the bridge with binoculars, but I didn't go out on a boat. If there was a body, I didn't want to remember my son that way.

WATER, WATER EVERYWHERE

IN JUNE 1989, TWO MONTHS into their dream of circumnavigating the globe, William and Simone Butler (right) were 1,200 miles southwest of Costa Rica when they spied a pod of whales. Soon they were in a nightmare straight out of *Moby Dick*: The whales attacked the Miami couple's 40-ft. sailboat, battering it so badly it began to take on water—fast. Scrambling into their rubber raft, they barely had time to grab a little food, fishing gear and a modest-looking device called the Survivor-35. Their first few anxious hours adrift turned to days, then weeks.

People can survive without fresh water for no more than a few days, yet the Butlers got

by—thanks to the Survivor-35 (right, bottom), a 7-lb. manually operated pump that forces seawater through a membrane that blocks the salt but passes the liquid. In the past, such systems had been too large and heavy for use on a lifeboat. But the year before the Butlers' voyage, a portable version was developed, and, luckily, they had one.

William, 59, squeezed three liters of water out of the device daily, and he and his wife survived 66 days until they were rescued by the Costa Rican coast guard. Simone, 51, who grew up near the French spa town of Evian, gave the Survivor's water quality a rave review: "Excellent. Just delicious."

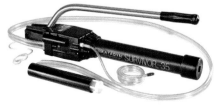

BEYOND MISERY

Stephen King, master of the macabre, was taking his daily walk when a van veered and his personal horror story began

TAKING A BREATHER from his work, author Stephen King set out on the afternoon of June 19, 1999, for a four-mile walk from his summer home in the mountain town of North Lovell, Maine. As he often did, King, 51, was reading a novel as he headed north against traffic on the two-lane Route 5. When the writer reached a hill where the shoulder narrowed, he closed the book, knowing that the blind stretch of road could be dangerous.

On the other side of the hill, heading south at about 45 mph, Bryan Smith, 42, a disabled former construction worker from the nearby town of Fryeburg, was driving a blue 1985 Dodge Caravan. Smith, who had been camping with a friend, was headed for town with his dog Bullet to load up his cooler. When Bullet started burrowing into it, Smith turned around and tussled with him. Seconds later, the van reached the crest of the hill, swerved off the pavement, then slammed into one of the world's best-read writers. "I went a little off the road," he said later. "I turned around, and I hit Stephen King, just bang-o!"

The van struck King on the right side with such force that his head shattered the windshield. Hurled over the vehicle, he landed in a grassy ditch 14 feet away. Lovell resident Donald Baker witnessed the accident from his pickup and immediately ran over to help. "I was surprised he was even alive," says Baker. "He was in a tangled-up mess, lying crooked, and had a heck of a gash on his head. He kept asking what had happened."

Because King's injuries were so severe—a shattered hip and pelvis, broken ribs and a fractured thighbone—a helicopter flew him to a trauma center in Lewiston, Maine, where in the next three weeks he endured six surgeries. About the only thing to escape injury was the author's mordant sense of humor, which kicked in almost from the moment of impact. After he hit the ground, King later told NBC's *Dateline,* "my entire waist was turned around sideways and I could see this bulge in the side of my jeans. And I thought to myself, 'If that's a bone, I'm in trouble here.'"

Returning to his mansion in Bangor, Maine, in July, racked with pain and unable to walk, King had a hospital bed set up in his ground-floor sunroom, where he passed the time playing catch with Marlowe, his 10-year-old corgi, and strumming his guitar. Writer Dave Barry, who

Six months after the accident, King, whose head broke the windshield of the van (left), went to the opening of *The Green Mile,* a film he wrote.

called King shortly after the accident, was shocked at how morose his friend had become. "He said, 'I thought I was gonna step out,'" Barry recalled. "He genuinely thought he was going to die."

For the next two months the wheelchair-bound King rarely ventured outside. On one occasion, he attended a reading by Maine author Tess Gerritsen. "Watching how much trouble it was to get him out of the van, I was so moved that he showed up," she said. By mid-October, King was well enough to go to Fenway Park in Boston to see his beloved Red Sox vie for a division title.

When King first returned to his craft, he was unable to sit without pain and could write only 90 minutes a day—a fraction of his normal four-hour stint. "Maybe there'll be another book, maybe there won't," he said on *Dateline.* "I'm more concerned with walking again without crutches."

The master chronicler of the sinister faced a regimen of physical therapy that would take years. Even then, doctors said, he might never regain full use of his right leg or walk without a cane. And, as King saw it, insult was heaped upon injury when Smith lost his driving rights for just one year and plea-bargained for a suspended six-month jail sentence for driving to endanger, thereby escaping the more serious charge of aggravated assault. "All in all, this has been the year from hell for Steve," King's friend Stu Tinker, owner of a bookstore in Bangor, said of 1999.

For his part, King denied bearing a grudge, saying the only thing he wanted was the permanent revocation of Smith's driver's license. "What he took from me—my time, my peace of mind, and my ease of body—are simply gone, and no court action can bring them back," King wrote in a letter to the court.

As if taken from a page in one of King's macabre tales, Smith was found dead in his trailer 15 months after the accident. He was just 43, though he suffered from various maladies that allowed him to walk only with crutches and required him to take seven medications daily. An autopsy determined the cause of death was an accidental overdose of the painkiller fentanyl. The news left King "feeling badly," said Warren Silver, the writer's attorney. "Smith is a sad figure for him, and it was just a tragic twist of fate that brought them together."

LOST AT SEA FOR 144 DAYS

Months after a storm crippled their boat, five Costa Rican fishermen arrive, alive, in Hawaii

Safely on land (from left), Juan Bolivar, Joel Gonzalez, Pastor Lopez, Jorge Hernandez and Gerardo Obregon celebrate. In the background is a boat similar to their abandoned *Cairo III*.

AT DAWN, JOEL GONZALEZ, 27, stood at the helm of the *Cairo III*, maneuvering the 30-ft. fishing boat through light Pacific swells. Suddenly the vessel shuddered, then lurched to one side. Within minutes a 50- to 60-mph squall struck with full force, heaving up three-story waves that bashed in doors and windows, swamped the cabin and left the wooden craft bobbing wildly. "There was so much noise, I thought the boat was breaking up," said Gonzalez, who was quickly joined on deck by his four panicked crewmates: Gerardo Obregon, 33, the skipper; Pastor Lopez, 27; Jorge Hernandez, 26; and Juan Bolivar, 47.

"The guys," said Gonzalez, "looked like monkeys, hanging on to anything they could grab. The boat was half filled with water, and we bailed like madmen. We lost our net, the radio went out, and before long the engine overheated and gave out. All day the water poured in. We'd nail the doors shut, but the waves would just smash them open again."

The *Cairo III* had been 20 miles off the coast of Costa Rica when the squall hit. When it failed to return, the coast guard launched a hunt—in vain. At sea the crew battled the weather for 22 days before the winds and water grew calm. By that point they were nearly out of food and swiftly losing hope. "We realized we had to depend on our own resources and couldn't expect help," Gonzalez recalled. "Right then we decided that we had to stick together. We made rules to ration fish we caught and water and agreed to bail in four-hour shifts."

They began dismantling the wooden cabin and its four sleeping berths to provide fuel for cooking. Still, they needed something to cook. All they had was a long, trailing fishing line with dangling hooks and no bait. As the waves abated, they decided to try to catch the turtles that inquisitively approached the boat. The turtles, some measuring up to three feet across, could be gaffed with a big hook tied to a pole.

"My job," Gonzalez explained, "was to hide

something were so small."

By late February, after about a month at sea, the men were drifting with the prevailing westerly winds and current. On a day of relative calm, Bolivar, whom the others nicknamed the Old Man, suggested they make a mast and sail. The only one among them who had worked on a sailboat, he volunteered to design and direct the project. "On our own, the way we are, we can't get anywhere," he said. "Only God could take us there, but it wouldn't hurt if we helped Him."

With a thick crossbeam wrenched out of the cabin roof, the men fashioned a 21-ft. mast, tore away planks to make a boom and sewed together blankets and pieces of vinyl cushion covers to create a crude, triangular sail. After the sail was fastened to the boom and mast with fishing line and wire, Bolivar had them make a rudder. The rudder worked well at first, but like the sail it had to be constantly repaired. Still, getting the boat back under way was a psychological boost and allowed the five to weather the storms they encountered.

On the morning of April 15—88 days in—as a few small birds flitted low over the foam-tipped swells, Hernandez was brushing his teeth near the stern when he looked up and saw a freighter about two miles away. "Look!" he shouted. "A ship! A ship!" For a long time the men shouted and waved their arms. Alas, no one aboard the freighter spotted the tiny speck of the *Cairo III* in the vast ocean, and the ship disappeared over the horizon. The men fell silent, their disappointment all the more acute because it was the second time a distant ship had passed them by. "We thought it was another of God's tests," said Lopez. "After that, we just assumed that we'd be saved or hit land if God meant us to."

behind the side rail and, before they could see me and be scared away, I'd have to spring up and hook them. As soon as we pulled one onto the deck, Gerardo would kill it and open the bottom part with his knife. Then Jorge would clean the meat, Pastor would cook us something like a stew in seawater, and Juan would divide up the pieces. I guess we trusted Juan the most to be fair. This was very important because some days we wouldn't catch anything, and when we finally did, even if it was a fish no bigger than a man's hand, it was Juan who'd cut up and distribute the little pieces."

After three weeks of waiting with no news from the coast guard, Gonzalez's and Obregon's wives Edith and Lydia hitched a two-hour ride to the capital city of San José. There they spoke with a government official who told them that the coast guard had been unable to search beyond the gulf because their large patrol boat had broken down. "He also said there were no clues about our husbands' whereabouts," Edith recalled, "and that they couldn't invest a lot of money on a search when the chances of finding

The day of that second boat sighting, Bolivar suffered a crippling attack of stomach pains. Although they all contended with constant diarrhea, the normally stoic Bolivar finally asked Gonzalez, the crew's "doctor," for some antacid pills. "I was the doctor only because I happened to bring along some aspirin and other pills," he said. "Poor Juan. He also had to have a tooth pulled, which we yanked out with a piece of twine."

Despite bailing around the clock, they had been riding ever lower in the water. In mid-May, Obregon ordered the engine to be dumped overboard to reduce the boat's weight and then dove in himself to plug holes and cracks in the hull. Wary of the sharks that circled with nerve-racking constancy, the others kept a close lookout while the captain stuffed rags and pieces of plastic and mattress sponge into the vessel's leaking skin.

On May 31, they once again rationed out the last dregs of water. Tormented by thirst, the men lay about on the deck in their tattered shorts, looking at the faraway, dark clouds that seemed to taunt them with the promise of rain. For four days they waited. Some thought of suicide, and all five passed into a kind of delirious stupor. But at their lowest ebb, Lopez gave a rousing talk to get the men moving again. "The sail was down, and we had been drifting," Lopez said. "I told them that God was tempting us to die the way the devil tempted Jesus. 'Fight back, get up and let's raise the sail!' I said. Somehow we did, and we started moving again."

As death became increasingly likely, the crew began to prepare. They even put on their best clothes, the ones they had been saving for their rescue. Then they lay down, closed their eyes and readied themselves. But after a while, a light rain began to fall. Their hopes reborn, the men became nearly hysterical with joy, licking moisture from the surface of the awning roof. "We were afraid it would stop," said Gonzalez, "but our prayers were answered, and it started to rain hard. At that point we were crying."

Ten days later, on the afternoon of June 15, a crewman on the bridge of the *Kinei Maru,* a Japanese fishing vessel, spotted the bobbing, sea-stained white hull of the *Cairo III.*

Gonzalez saw the ship first. "I'd just caught a shark when I looked up and saw it," he says. "I remember saying, 'Hey, a boat! A boat!' and screaming to them to wave to it. We were all leaping with joy." Their ordeal was over.

Having endured 144 days at sea and drifted 4,000 miles from Costa Rica, the five survivors were taken to Honolulu, where a U.S. Army doctor examined them and found them surprisingly fit. When the men arrived back in Costa Rica, they were given a hero's welcome, especially in Puntarenas, their point of departure. There, after the five shared tears and hugs with their families, hundreds of cheering fishermen and other townsfolk paraded them through the streets.

"I never thought I'd see my wife and kids again," said Gonzalez. "That's why I started to write her a note on the boat explaining how we died. I kept it in a little bottle with my gold ring tied to the top. With my last strength, I was going to throw the bottle into the water, hoping someone would find it and send her the note."

He wrote: "Edith, don't spend the rest of your life suffering and wondering what happened to me.... I fought till the end and did everything I could to return to you. But finally I was defeated.... I only know one thing—that if it's possible to love after life, I will love you."

> 66 I'd just caught a shark when I looked up and saw it. I remember saying, 'Hey, a boat! A boat!' and screaming to them to wave"

Loved ones reunited: "It was as if God had shown me the way back to my family," said Gonzalez (left, with his wife, Edith; at center is the letter he wrote her at sea). "These men are heroes," said Hilda Rojas (right, with her son Pastor Lopez).

CHAPTER 4

ADVENTURERS

THERE'S A THRILL—AND THERE'S A RISK

The crew of the *Nokia* fought violent seas in the race from Sydney to the island of Tasmania. "Man is no match for the fury of the ocean," said a competitor.

MAN OVERBOARD

A sudden storm turned an Australian yacht race into a life-and-death battle

"IT WAS A BEAUTIFUL *spinnaker run down the coast," sailor John Flannery recalled of the opening stage of Australia's 1998 Sydney to Hobart, Tasmania, yacht race. Almost 26 hours later, leaders of the 725-mile, 115-yacht race ran head-on into a shrieking gale with 90-mph winds that churned walls of water up to 80 feet high.*

MIKE MARSHMAN, 45, crew member aboard the yacht *VC Offshore Stand Aside*: Coming down the coast that first day, we were high as kites, absolutely flying. We were racing pretty much in the kind of weather we expected. We thought there would be 50-knot winds. But within half an hour, they turned and were up to 75. Then the waves! They were huge. If someone had told me, I'd have said, "Bull----, waves don't get this big!" Now we know they do.

PETER JOUBERT, 74, of Melbourne, owner and skipper of the *Kingurra*: It was heading toward evening [Sun., Dec. 27] and the winds were screaming. It was an absolute maelstrom, like a scene from hell. I was asleep at the time the first big wave hit; then I found myself being flung about in the cabin. We were vertical. I was breathless, and I knew I had broken some ribs.

We got a pump going—there must have been three or four tons of water in the boat. I could hear these cries from the

cockpit: "We've got men overboard!" They got one fellow back—two people pulled him in by his safety line. Two others tried to pull John Campbell in, but his arms slipped right out of his life jacket. In the meantime, I'm on the radio saying, "Mayday! Mayday! Mayday!" There was so much foam in the sea you couldn't see anything. I told the crew to throw the [emergency] beacon overboard, hoping it would float near John.

Slowly I started to realize that I was actually swimming in the ocean and that I was in significant trouble.

MELISSA McCABE, 18, Australian high school student who won a berth as a deckhand on the *Team Jaguar Infinity III* by winning an essay competition: People were being sick. When the wave hit, the deck above me cracked. It was like a waterfall in the middle of the boat.

JOHN FLANNERY, 30, aboard the *Nokia*: Even though we were the

by a huge wave. The boom came flying across the deck and hit the wheel. Glyn [Charles] was steering at the time. We all wonder if the wheel didn't crash into him. He was flung off the ship without his safety harness—it snapped with the impact of the wave. Within 30 seconds, he was nearly 100 meters from us. There wasn't a thing we could do. We had all the rescue equipment overboard within 30 seconds, but we were drifting rapidly away from

JOHN CAMPBELL, 32, of Seattle, crew member on the *Kingurra*: An extremely large wave came crashing onto the deck, the boat rolled, and I hit my chin pretty hard. I was completely unconscious. When the boat righted itself, I was dragging behind it by my harness. My friend Peter [Meikle] went to work trying to pull me out of the drink, and he managed all by himself to hoist me up. But he couldn't get me over the lifeline. Suddenly I slipped right out of my jacket and my harness. I slipped out of Peter's grasp.

I came to in the water and saw the boat a quarter to a half mile away. I have this memory of debating with myself whether this was all a dream.

biggest boat out there, a lot of us were just getting flung bodily from one side of the boat to the other. We were hit by a wave, and I was thrown 20 feet across the other side of the boat. The radio was a mess. There were maydays and distress calls everywhere. Flares popping up all over the place. It was berserk.

CARL WATSON, 44, of Sydney, a helmsman aboard the *Sword of Orion*, whose crew included British Olympian Glyn Charles, 33: We told the radio ship *Endeavour* that we were getting 70- to 75-knot winds. When that information was relayed back to the rest of the fleet, many of them decided to turn back. Almost two hours later, we got hit

him. We never saw him again.

CAMPBELL, in the sea off the stern of the *Kingurra*: All my energies were focused on doing whatever I could to get back to the boat or try to get them to spot me. I had no idea if they knew where I was. I was yelling out but realized that there was no way they could hear me with the wind. It was this screeching, deafening howling. As they got farther and farther away, my hopes of surviving were starting to fade.

KRISTY McALISTER, 30, of Canberra, paramedic on the SouthCare ambulance helicopter, as she prepared to be lowered into the sea on a safety harness to rescue two men: I was petrified. It was my first sea rescue, there wasn't a lot of visibility, and there were 60-to-70-ft. waves. I just looked at the sea and thought, "Oh. My. God." On my first winch down, just as I was hitting the water, one of the waves came in, and I was dumped under the water for quite some time before I came up. Eventually I made it to the surface and made my way as best I could to a man who was floating separate from the life raft.

I take my hat off to the other para-

way. As he tried to get up, he had a seizure and died [from a heart attack] in my arms.

MARK RUDIGER, 44, navigator for the *Sayonara*: Everybody was getting really tired, sore, bruised and beat up. At that point we were concentrating on trying to get the boat safely through this weather. We weren't really racing. We never thought about quitting. For us, the safest and fastest way out of the system was to continue the direction we were

CLAY, 37, winch operator on the Victoria police Air Wing rescue helicopter: We got a message from the rescue center to track toward the *Kingurra*, and I knew we could get there in 10 minutes. *Kingurra* gave us an approximate position to where the man overboard was. It was in fading light. We saw one of the life rings first, but there was no one there. Then out of the corner of my eye, I saw something that wasn't supposed to be there. It was John.

John Campbell (far left) suffered hypothermia before being plucked from the sea; the *Nokia* (center) nearly capsized; Melissa McCabe, who earned a spot on one of the yachts through a contest, greeted her grandmother after making a safe landing.

" The waves! They were huge. If someone had told me, I'd have said, 'Bull----, waves don't get this big!' Now we know they do"

medic, Peter Davidson. He did eight rescues by himself, and I was exhausted after two. With the freak waves coming in, it was quite difficult for our pilot as well: At one stage the chopper was 60 feet above the water, but when the wave came in he was only 10 feet above it.

STEVE WALKER, 45, crew member of the *Business Post Naiad*, which had capsized with Tasmanian skipper Bruce Guy, 51, and his neighbor Phil Skeggs, 34: We heard Rob [Matthews] calling for Phil [who, when the boat overturned, had been pulled underwater and drowned]. We didn't hear Phil answer and couldn't do anything about it. Bruce was beside the main hatch-

heading, toward the finish line. The weather was worse behind us.

CAMPBELL, of the *Kingurra*, who had been in the water for nearly 40 minutes and was beginning to suffer the effects of hypothermia: There was a point I didn't think I was going to survive. I don't recall specifically getting really tired or thinking I couldn't go on any longer—I just tried to swim toward the boat when I saw it. The next real strong image that I have is a flare going up on the boat, and I couldn't understand why they were doing that. But moments after that, I heard the helicopter screaming over my head. I was elated.

SENIOR CONSTABLE BARRY BAR-

CAMPBELL: I was waving my arms frantically, just trying to get their attention. They did a fantastic job of putting someone close to me. After talking to the rescue guys later, I realized what a challenge that must have been. When I got up in the helicopter, I kept saying, "Thank you."

DAVID ROUT, 66, *Kingurra* crew member: They told us they pulled John out, but we didn't know then if it was a body. Then we got another message to say he was alive, and our spirits went up 200-fold.

PETER MEIKLE, 32, *Kingurra* crew member: I had told John that if he raced this year, I'd guarantee that he'd make it to Hobart or I'd pay his airfare home. It's a small price.

"I'm stronger for what I went through," said LeMarque, who lost both feet.

EIGHT DAYS IN THE SNOW
Snowboarder Eric LeMarque swooped into the trees—and almost didn't return

SNOWBOARDER ERIC LEMARQUE had just broken up with his girlfriend, so he was a little distracted when he headed up the slopes of the Mammoth Mountain ski resort in California. "I figured three hours of riding and then I'd hit the Jacuzzi," said LeMarque, 35.

On his last run he decided to take a secluded trail. Fog and darkness closed in, and before he knew it, he was lost. He knew that temperatures would soon drop into the single digits; he also knew that if he tried to find his way out in the dark he'd probably only make his situation worse. Using his snowboard as a shovel, he dug a rudimentary

snow cave and took stock of his supplies: a dead cell phone and an MP3 player. No food. For dinner, he munched on pine nuts and bark.

The next morning, he walked toward what he hoped was safety. Unfortunately, he wound up deeper in the woods. His feet had begun to hurt. Shucking his boots and socks, he was horrified to find his toes blackened and bleeding. "I knew I had to get out of there," he says.

For the seven agonizing days that followed, LeMarque used radio signals he picked up on his MP3 as a sort of compass to steer himself on a consistent course. Still, each day was a struggle, and he covered only a few

hundred yards at a time. For two days he was so exhausted he mainly slept. Just when he thought things couldn't get worse, he looked up to find himself surrounded by coyotes. He screamed, and kept screaming, until they ran off. It wasn't until the eighth day that a helicopter rescue crew finally found him.

Suffering from severe frostbite, hypothermia and dehydration, LeMarque lost each leg six inches below the knee. Four months later, after having been fitted with prosthetic feet, he walked down the aisle with Sheri Van Den Eikhof, the girlfriend he had split with before embarking on his misadventure.

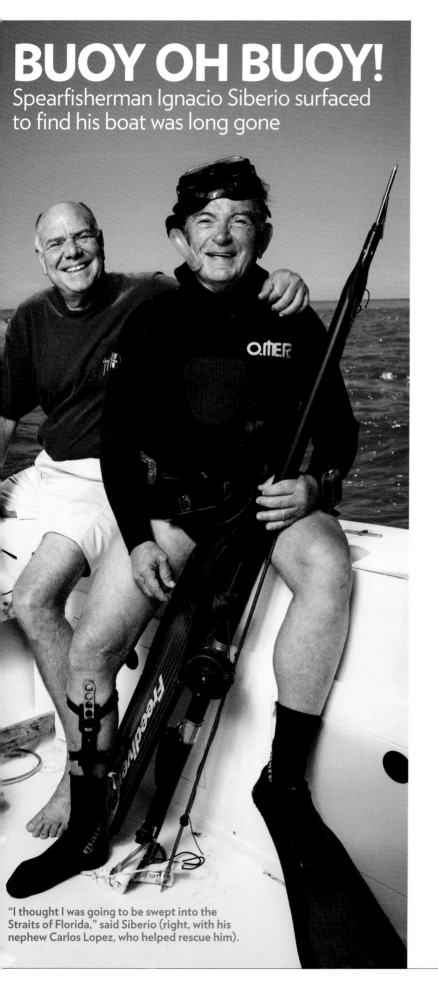

BUOY OH BUOY!

Spearfisherman Ignacio Siberio surfaced to find his boat was long gone

"I thought I was going to be swept into the Straits of Florida," said Siberio (right, with his nephew Carlos Lopez, who helped rescue him).

LOOKING BACK, Ignacio Siberio knew he had made a number of imperfect decisions. The winds were gusty and the water choppy, but he took his 25-ft. sailboat out anyway. Worse, even though his two regular spearfishing buddies couldn't join him, Siberio, 80, decided to make the seven-mile trip off the Florida Keys by himself. It was Dec. 11, 2004, and, Siberio admitted later, "I shouldn't have been there."

Still, he donned his fins, mask and the top of his wet suit, snatched up his speargun and jumped over the side. For three hours, he chased fish of all kinds but came up empty. Frustrated, he decided to head home. But there was a problem. "When I came to the surface, I looked around and the boat was gone," he said. A storm had moved in, bringing violent winds that had apparently dislodged the boat's anchors and sent it adrift. Desperate to catch up with it, Siberio dug into the swift current and swam for his life.

He swam for hours but made little progress. Then he got a break: There, floating atop the waves, were five 1-ft.-long buoys tied together. "It was a miracle," he said. He swam to them and held on. As night fell, Siberio tried to keep his mind off of his desperate plight by thinking about his family and the ongoing cases at his law firm.

When he failed to return to port that evening, his fishing buddies—his nephew Carlos Lopez and friend Roberto Garcia —contacted the Coast Guard. They found nothing that evening and set out again early the next morning, heading straight for Siberio's favorite fishing spots. Battling heaving seas, Garcia and Lopez decided to venture farther from land and saw an astonishing sight. "He had cut the buoys and wrapped them around him and was swimming," says Lopez.

Pulling up alongside the rescue boat, Siberio climbed aboard. As exhausted as he was, he refused to go to a hospital. Upon arriving at his Tavernier, Fla., weekend home, he was greeted by loved ones led by his wife, Gloria, 68. Despite his scare, he has since been spearfishing several times. "My lesson is you have to be careful," he says.

CHOOSING TO LIVE

His arm trapped by a rock, climber Aron Ralston slowly ran out of options. Alone and desperate, he took out his knife and began to cut

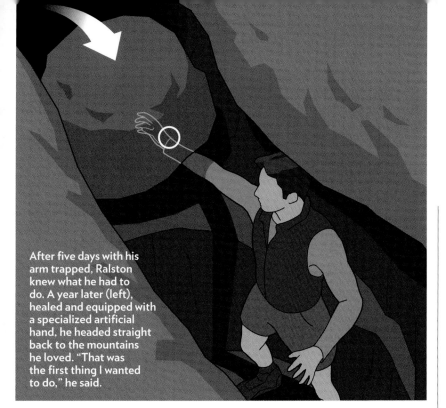

After five days with his arm trapped, Ralston knew what he had to do. A year later (left), healed and equipped with a specialized artificial hand, he headed straight back to the mountains he loved. "That was the first thing I wanted to do," he said.

ALL ARON RALSTON HAD in mind was a weekend break from his job at an Aspen, Colo., mountaineering store. As he had done so often before, he decided to go for a serious hike. This is a guy who had climbed all 54 of the state's 14,000-ft.-plus peaks. Loading his mountain bike into his truck, he headed for Horseshoe Canyon in southeastern Utah, parked the truck and rode off.

Fifteen miles in, he left the bike and proceeded on foot. Minutes later, while climbing alone in barren Bluejohn Canyon, Ralston, 28, was descending, without ropes, through a steep slot between two rock faces. He began to navigate a 10-foot drop between ledges when a massive 800-lb. stone suddenly shifted. The rock came came down hard, pinning his right hand against the ledge. He shoved with every ounce of his strength but couldn't free himself. "The adrenaline was pumping very, very hard," he later said. "It took some calm thinking to get myself to stop throwing myself against the boulder."

The time: 2:45 on Saturday afternoon, April 26, 2003. Ralston knew the situation was dire. A desert rainstorm, common at that time of year, could flash-flood the canyon, drowning him on the spot. With only a liter of water, Ralston also feared dehydration.

Mentally, he ticked off his options, none of them good: He could hope that someone would wander down the remote trail. He could try, somehow, with ropes and leverage, to move the rock. Or he could try to chip away at the boulder and make an opening big enough for his hand to slip out. There was one, last, too-awful-to contemplate option: He could cut off his own arm.

As the days slipped by—one, two, three—with no other hikers and no success at freeing himself, Ralston made a harrowing choice. "On Tuesday morning," he said, "I took my pocket knife." After preparing a tourniquet and carefully rehearsing his anticipated movements, he put the blade to his arm and began sawing back and forth. Nothing happened: the blade was too dull. He stopped, and decided to wait some more.

On the sixth day, dehydrated and fading in and out of consciousness, Ralston probed his wounds and discovered the flesh was beginning to rot. It would only be a matter of time before infection overcame him. At the discovery, he grew furious with his own hand and, rather than fearing amputation, he longed for it.

Resolved to finish the job, he decided it might be easier to cut through the flesh if he could first break the bones. It wasn't easy; he needed leverage. By twisting and turning himself, he found a strong position—and snapped his radius and, a few minutes later, the thinner ulna, at the wrist.

Using his dull knife, he opened a four-inch gash in the skin. Fearing he might cut the arteries too soon and bleed to death before he could apply a tourniquet, he clamped his knife in his teeth and, with his fingers, dug into the opening to identify the muscle, tendons and ligaments that he would sever first. Only at the end would he cut the arteries. As for the sometimes searing sensations, he said, "I felt pain and I coped with it." Finally, he was free.

Friends and authorities had been searching for days for Ralston when a helicopter spotted two hikers waving frantically. With them was a man with his right arm in a makeshift sling. As the pilot touched down, Ralston approached and told him calmly, "I'm the one you're looking for."

Several surgeries followed, and Ralston was ultimately fitted with a prosthetic hand with attachments for every activity from biking to climbing. As for his original, the helicopter crew had little trouble finding the blood-splashed rock, though they had to leave the hand behind. Three days later, it took a crew of 13 an hour to lift the boulder and recover his hand. As soon as he was able, Ralston returned to the mountains, both because he still loved to climb and because he had a special mission. At the spot where he had been trapped, he said a final goodbye to his hand and scattered its ashes into the canyon.

HANGING TOUGH

In an instant, Bethany Hamilton lost an arm to a shark she never saw

IT WAS A PERFECT DAY—another perfect day—in paradise for 13-year-old Bethany Hamilton and her surfing buddies. An amateur champion whose prowess had earned her corporate sponsorships from surf-wear companies like Rip Curl and put her on track for a pro career, Bethany was floating on her board off the Hawaiian island of Kauai on Halloween Day, 2003. "She was paddling in, not really trying to catch a wave, just playing and making little happy, squeaky noises," says Jeff Walba, 52, who was with Hamilton and half a dozen fellow surfers about 200 yards offshore when she was attacked by what authorities believed was a 14- to 15-ft. 1-ton tiger shark—although the animal struck so quickly, not one of the nearby surfers saw it. "There wasn't even a ripple. She thrust her hand down into a wave, and then her arm was gone."

"It's funny—you would think having your arm bitten off would really hurt," Hamilton wrote in her 2004 memoir, *Soul Surfer*. "But there was no pain at the time." Recalled Walba: "She never screamed. She said, 'Shark,' but didn't freak."

While Walba made for shore to call for help, Holt Blanchard, 49, the father of Bethany's best friend, Alana, 13, applied a tourniquet fashioned from a surfboard leash to stop the bleeding. His quick thinking—plus the fact that Bethany was in peak physical condition—almost certainly saved her life. "The biggest risks with shark bites are blood loss and shock," said a shark expert at the Hawaii Institute of Marine Biology. Following surgery at Kauai's Wilcox Memorial Hospital, the surfer girl had one request: "I want to get back in the water."

And so she did. Less than three months after the attack, Hamilton was working out on a customized surfboard and competing in tournaments. Though fit with a prosthesis, she surfs without covering "Stumpy," her name for the $1\frac{1}{2}$-in. stump that is all that remains of her arm. Brave as she is, she avoids Tunnels Beach, where she was attacked. "There are enough beaches in Kauai," she says.

"I didn't believe I was going to survive," said Simpson (left, in '02) of his ordeal on Siula Grande (opposite page). Said Yates (in hat): "I [made] an instant, instinctive decision—'I'm going to cut the rope.'"

ON JUNE 8, 1985, *British climbers Joe Simpson and Simon Yates became the first to scale the west face of Siula Grande, a 21,000-ft. Andean peak 250 miles from Lima, Peru. Standing on the snowy summit, Simpson, then 25, and Yates, 21, had little time to savor the rush: A blizzard loomed, so they started hastily down the mountain.*

Despite the storm, Simpson and Yates descended the first 3,000 feet without incident. Then, as Simpson negotiated an ice wall, his axe slipped and he fell 15 feet, breaking his right leg. "Simon had a choice of leaving me there to die or helping me," he says. "He chose to help." Until that point, the pair had climbed alpine-style, tied together. Now Yates used the ropes to lower Simpson down the mountain, 300 feet at a time.

For nine exhausting hours, and 3,000 feet, it worked. Then Simpson, inching down a slope, began to slide. The rope between the two men went taut and Yates attempted to brake Simpson's fall, but it was too late. Simpson went over a cliff, where he dangled 50 feet over a gaping crevasse. Yates, above him but out of view, anchoring the other end of the rope with his body and all of his strength, couldn't hear Simpson's cries over the roar of the wind. Yates tried desperately for an hour to raise his friend, but could do nothing. His strength draining and the snow

beneath him giving way, he faced a horrible choice: cut the rope, or slide over the cliff himself. He took out a penknife. "Then," Simpson says, "I just fell."

Plummeting into the crevasse, he landed on a small bridge of ice. There he lay, in a dark, eerily silent hole, more alone than he ever thought possible. "I cried like a baby," says Simpson, who remarkably suffered no additional injuries in the fall. "I had to regain control to have any chance of getting out." Unable to climb up and with a limited supply of rope, he could only crawl deeper into the void. About 80 feet down, he saw a glimmer of light. After crawling toward it for two agonizing hours he poked his head through the glacier and into open air. It was, he says, "the most stupendous view I had ever seen."

Meanwhile, Yates was making his way down the mountain, convinced Simpson was dead and that he too would perish.

Simpson's ordeal was just beginning. Slowly, he edged across the vast glacier, using his arms and good leg to drag the broken leg, its fractured bones shifting with every inch. The pain was murderous. Freezing and weak, with no food or unfrozen water, he lost his bearings several times. "I knew I wasn't going to make it, so why not just sit there and die?" he says. "But I had a sickening sense of loneliness. I think that's what made me keep going."

At the end of the glacier, six miles of jagged rocks lay between Simpson and safety. He set 20-minute goals, keeping time on a $4 watch. Delirious, he heard old songs in his head and started reciting Shakespeare. He had crawled eight miles in total, but even with an end almost in sight, he was finally cracking.

Then, as he dragged himself along at 3 a.m. on June 12, the unmistakable aroma of urine and excrement snapped him back to reality. Four days after being left for dead, he had made it to the base camp latrine. He cried weakly for help

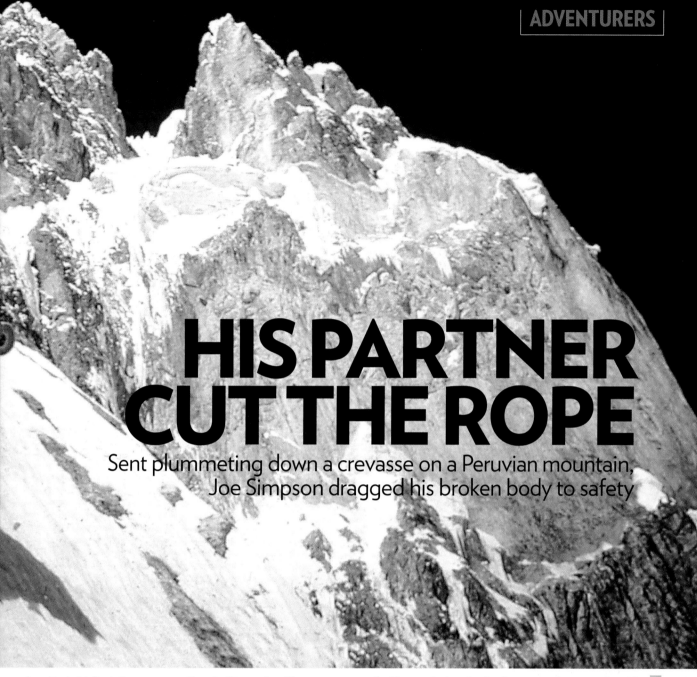

HIS PARTNER CUT THE ROPE

Sent plummeting down a crevasse on a Peruvian mountain, Joe Simpson dragged his broken body to safety

and waited. At first there was nothing. Then he looked up and a disbelieving Yates appeared with Richard Hawking, a friend who had watched over their camp while they climbed.

"You imagine you'll be all heroic and say something like 'Hello, Simon. I've had a bit of a rough time,'" Simpson says. "But I was so tired, I was in so much pain, I just started crying."

Yates, who made it back to camp in a day, had been racked with guilt. "If Joe hadn't crawled back into camp," he later told Britain's *Times*, "it would have been horrendous. I was still in a chronic state of shock."

Strapping Simpson to a mule, Yates and Hawking headed for Lima and the nearest hospital. It was a two-day ride, plus 20 hours in the back of a pickup, but they made it.

In England, Yates came under withering criticism from some in the climbing community for abandoning Simpson. Friendly but not close, the pair kept in touch over the years. In 1988, Simpson published his chronicle of the events in a book titled *Touching the Void*, later made into a documentary by Oscar-winning director Kevin Macdonald. The film brought the two together again, but just briefly. "In context you real-

ize he had to cut the rope," said Macdonald. "[But] if you've done something you're not particularly proud of, you don't want to be known for it for the rest of your life."

Through it all, Simpson staunchly defended Yates, calling him a hero for even attempting a rescue. "It was a feat of extraordinary strength and determination," he says. "People ask, 'Would you have cut the rope in Simon's position?' Of course I would have. He made the incredibly brave decision to save me. But he's known as the guy who cut the rope, and I'm the guy who crawled out and wrote the book."

THE DOUBLE WHAMMY

Actor Tony Danza broke his back skiing.
He was still recovering when the earthquake hit

A year after ending his eight-season run on *Who's the Boss?*, Danza (working out at home) suffered a near-fatal fall on a Utah ski run (above).

ON THE MORNING of Dec. 28, 1993, perennial TV star Tony Danza, then 42, was vacationing at his mountain retreat in Deer Valley, Utah, with his wife, Tracy, then 34, their daughters Katie, 6, and Emily Lyn, 1 month, and Marc, his 22-year-old son by his first marriage. At 9 a.m., when the hills were still shrouded in fog, Danza headed for the top of the mountain for his first ski run of the day.

The snow covering was hard-packed and icy. Danza got only about 100 yards down Birdseye, an intermediate trail he had skied hundreds of times, when he skidded out of control. "It wasn't like I panicked," he said. "I remember thinking, 'Okay, get your feet in front and stop yourself.' That's the last thing I remember."

He fell, lost his skis and slammed backward into a tree. His injuries were massive: two broken vertebrae, crushed ribs, a collapsed lung and a bruised liver and kidney. His right leg pulled out of the hip socket. "It was like having a car accident," said Danza, "without the car."

The ski patrol arrived within minutes and he was loaded onto a sleigh. Terrified he'd be paralyzed, Danza was relieved that he felt some sensation in his ski boot. He was rushed by ambulance to Park City Medical Center and eventually transferred to the University of Utah Hospital in Salt Lake City, where a team of spinal specialists decided to operate as soon as he stopped bleeding internally. Tracy stayed close by for his three weeks in the hospital. "He didn't want me to leave," she says, "and I couldn't. We were both very scared."

In a four-hour operation on New Year's Day, surgeons inserted three metal rods into Danza's lower back. Afterward he was in intensive care for two weeks and dropped 25 lbs. from his 5'11", 165-lb. frame before embarking on what would become a painful, yearlong physical-therapy regimen. "I tried to be the best patient ever," he says. "I really had trouble thinking about what my life would be like if I wasn't me anymore."

But before he could start rehab, Danza had to face another crisis. Still dependent on a walker, he left the hospital and returned to his Sherman Oaks, Calif., home on Jan. 14, 1994.

Three days later, the 6.6 magnitude Northridge earthquake hit. "The house exploded," recalled Danza, who was sleeping upstairs when the quake struck at 4:31 a.m. "The bed almost hit the ceiling. I just hung on to Tracy."

His daughters' bedroom wall collapsed; the girls made it out with the help of a housekeeper. Danza followed downstairs with his walker. "He was pretty amazing," says Tracy.

With their house in ruins, the family relocated to a rental home, then moved permanently to their Malibu beach house. What lesson did Danza glean from those eventful weeks?

"It's called the present," he said "because it's a gift."

CHAPTER 5

ACCIDENTS

AN ORDINARY DAY, UNTIL SOMETHING GOES WRONG

ON FEB. 20, 2003, *minutes after the heavy-metal band Great White took the stage at the Station, a club in West Warwick, R.I., the band's pyrotechnic display sent flames rushing through the cramped space. Suddenly 350 panicked fans faced a wall of fire, and there were only four exit doors to safety. Survivors, rescuers and relatives recalled the scene:*

MICHAEL RICARDI, 19, student: After the pyro went off, a foam insulation backdrop caught fire. It looked like it was part of the show at first. Then the bassist looked back and stopped playing and went through the side door; the guitarist dropped his guitar and ran. Then [frontman] Jack Russell looked and said, "This isn't good." From there it was just total mayhem.

LISA SHEA, 31, clothing-store manager: I thought the fire was part of the act. I said to my friend, "Be calm." But then, when the top of the front of the stage started flaming, I said, "No, something is going on." At the front door it looked like an arrow of people—everyone smushed in. I said, "We'll never get over there." The house lights were on, but then the fire got worse and they went out. When that happened and the smoke got worse, everybody panicked. I fell to the floor. I was panicking, but I yelled, "Can everyone just calm down?"

ERIN MARIE PUCINO, 25, secretary: We got about two to three feet from the door, and that's when everybody fell over in front of us. Then we fell over them. . . . The smoke started surrounding us. I kept trying to put my jacket and sweater over my mouth, but the smoke came right through.

SHEA: People were walking on my back and my head. The black smoke was everywhere, and I just

NIGHTCLUB INFERNO

Pyrotechnics at a Great White
concert set off a horrifying fire

At the beginning of their
show, Great White set off
fireworks to excite the
crowd (far left). Within
moments, soundproofing
foam around the stage
caught fire and fans panicked.
"I knew if I stayed there I
was going to die," said one.
The Station club (above)
was reduced to rubble.

thought, "I'm going to die here." Then I thought of my mother and got the will to get up and yelled, "Will everyone get off of me!" People were screaming. I got up and put my hand on the person in front of me. That person moved and I saw a light. It was a window, so I leaped out.

CHRIS TRAVIS, 37, construction worker: I got knocked down, and lost my sense of direction. I couldn't remember where the exit was. And it was like being blind—I couldn't even see my hand in front of my face. People were tripping and falling on top of me. I had no idea which way to go. I decided to follow in the direction of the people who were tripping over me. So I pulled my jacket over my head so I could breathe and walked on my hands and knees.

PUCINO: When we fell, we were halfway in and half out the door. Two girls who were standing on the ground in front of the steps were trying to pull me out. They just didn't have enough leverage. They kept saying, "Don't worry, we're going to get you out." But my legs were under so many people that they just couldn't.

TRAVIS: I could see people throwing anything they could through the windows, trying to get out and jumping. There were people covered in blood and on fire, clothes burned and skin just melting and hanging. People were running out of the main entrance in a ball of fire. They were trying to roll in the snow.

PUCINO: As those two girls were trying to pull me out, this man grabbed my arms and kept trying to pull. I said, "Please keep pulling, I think I'm moving." He kept pulling and pulling, and then he did pull me out—right before the flames started coming through the door.

STEPHEN EARLEY, 46, an artist who came to offer help: People outside were burnt black, and I was trying to sit and pray with them while they got the rescue squads. Suddenly I came across my sister Sharon, except I didn't recognize her. She ran toward me, and I was thinking, "Oh

"It was like Judgment Day for us," said a concert goer who was able to escape the wall of flames.

my God, who's this?" It was her, she was on fire, burning. She was smoldering, and she had burning pieces in her hair.

JUDY O'BRIEN, 50, happened to be driving near the Station, where she knew her son Robert Reisner, 29, a school bus driver, had gone to see the show: When you are thinking, "Where is my son?" you don't even really know what's happening around you. They let us into the Cowesett Inn, across from the Station, and we just waited there. I had some hope.

JIMMY PAOLUCCI, 41, owner of the Cowesett Inn: The first guy in was in his underwear. His clothes either burned off or he took them off. He was saying, "Take other people first." He was very upset, shaking and dumping buckets of water over his head. As the stretcher was coming in to move people out, he pointed over to a girl and said, "Why don't you take her first?" The girl was lying on the floor. You could see the pain he was in, shaking.

PETER GINAITT, 42, rescue worker: I would look at their faces, and if their hair was burnt off their head and they have facial burns, then you know they have taken in that 1000° or 1200° heat, so they actually have singed lungs. Those are the people who, even though they are breathing

right now, in 20 minutes they are going to have respiratory distress; in 30 minutes they are going to have to be intubated in order to breathe.

DR. MICHAEL DACEY, 38: I grew up five minutes from here. The people who you treat are your neighbors, friends, people you know from Little League. There was a time during those four hours when everyone quietly said to themselves that if we had a say, nobody else was going to die. I felt my whole career was preparation for this one night.

O'BRIEN: My son Rob was one of the first seven [dead] identified. The person from the Red Cross sat us down and told all of us on Saturday morning... I had to pick out a casket for my son today. When you pick out a crib, it's life. When you pick out a casket to put your child in, it's the end. It's horrible. It's not fair.

The tragedy left 100 dead and almost 200 injured. Among those who didn't make it was Great White guitarist Ty Longley, 31. His mother, Mary Pat Fredericksen, 53, said he was a sensitive young man: "I called him an old soul because he was so spiritual. Whenever Christmas happened, he cried when he got his presents, he would weep with happiness. He would always write Santa Claus a thank-you note."

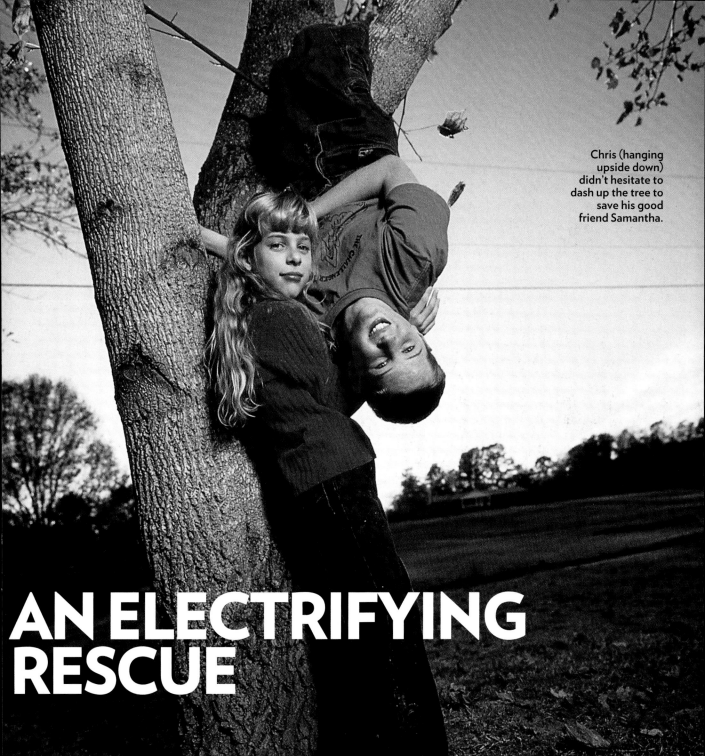

Chris (hanging upside down) didn't hesitate to dash up the tree to save his good friend Samantha.

AN ELECTRIFYING RESCUE

IT BEGAN WITH A DARE. When her cousin bet her a dollar that she couldn't climb a neighbor's 40-ft. elm, Samantha Edwards, 9, promptly accepted and scrambled up into the tree. It only took her a few minutes to reach the top and crow in triumph. "But when I started down," the Lincolnton, N.C., fourth grader recalled of that afternoon in July of 2001, "I slipped, and my sandal got caught."

Then things got worse. As neighborhood kids described it, there was a sudden sound like "bees and beetles fighting," then "a flash of blue," and "Samantha screaming." Her playmates looked up to see her dangling upside

down by one foot. Samantha had touched a power line in the tree and been jolted with a 7,200-volt blast of electricity.

Before nearby adults realized what was happening, neighbor Chris Haney, 11, barefoot and wearing only shorts, shinnied up the tree. "I was afraid she was going to fall," said the Boy Scout. "I didn't want her to die." In minutes Haney reached the still-conscious girl and ordered her to grab his neck. "Her leg looked burned," he said. "She had to hold on with her elbows because her hands were all black."

Maneuvering his way down through thick branches, Chris, carrying Saman-

tha, made it back to terra firma just as emergency workers arrived. They rushed her to nearby Lincoln Medical Center, where she was listed in critical condition with second- and third-degree burns. She later received skin grafts on her arm, leg and foot but suffered no internal injuries.

Local emergency crew members marveled at Chris's courage. "A lot of folks trained in rescue work couldn't have done what he did," said spokesman Josh Wagner. But a chivalrous Chris gave credit for the successful rescue to his friend. "Samantha is a powerful dude," he said with a smile. "Well, dude-ette."

TIGER TERROR!

In an instant, the huge white tiger Ray Horn had raised since birth had him by the throat

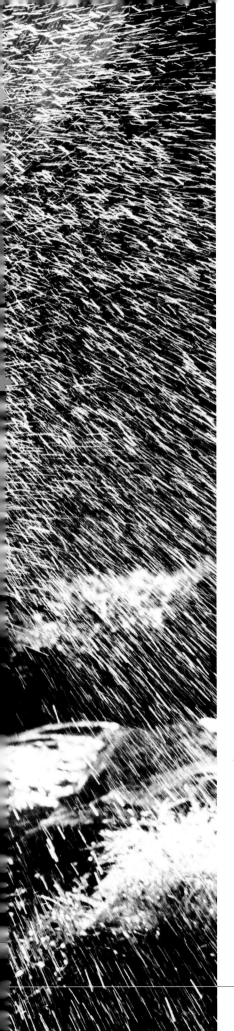

"He instinctively saw that I needed help, and he helped me," said Horn (above, with Montecore in 2002, before the incident). The tiger still lives in a Mirage zoo.

IT WAS YET ANOTHER FULL HOUSE at the Siegfried & Roy Theatre at the Mirage in Las Vegas. The tightly paced 95-minute extravaganza—costumed dancers, a laser light show, a mechanical dragon, the illusions performed by Siegfried Fischbacher and those gorgeous white Bengal tigers and white lions trained by Roy Horn—was running like clockwork. It was during one of the least spectacular segments of the show that Horn came onstage with one of the white tigers, a 7-year-old male named Montecore, to explain his work preserving these rare animals. Ordinarily, Montecore lies down, then stands with his paws on Horn's shoulders and gives him a sort of embrace. Not this night.

Instead, said a fan who witnessed what followed, the normally placid Montecore unexpectedly growled. Horn chided it—"No, no"—and pulled on the tiger's chain. "Roy told the tiger to lay down," said another audience member, "and he didn't."

Las Vegas mogul Steve Wynn, former owner of the Mirage, said Fischbacher believed Montecore was somehow distracted by a woman up front. Horn swiftly moved to block Montecore's view and get him to return to their well-rehearsed script. At that point Montecore grabbed Horn's arm with his forepaws—or possibly with his mouth, said one fan. Horn disciplined Montecore by bopping him on the nose with a microphone once, twice, as many as five times. Then, Horn stumbled, and the cat pounced, biting into Roy's neck.

Seconds later, reverting to routine, Montecore exited stage left. But on this night—Oct. 3, 2003—he dragged the 59-year-old Horn out by the throat. Backstage, the crew—trained for such an incident, the first in a career that spanned 30,000 performances, says the pair's manager—sprayed the cat with a fire extinguisher. Releasing Horn, Montecore retired to his cage, then was whisked back to the Mirage's small zoo.

The audience, meanwhile, was stunned, unsure whether what they had seen could possibly have been part of the act. Ten-year-old Quentin Rohrbacher, a visitor from Britain, sank his face into his mother's sleeve. "I tried to tell him it would be okay and that it wasn't real because this was supposed to be magic," said Mary Alice Rohrbacher, 40. But then Siegfried returned, visibly distraught, and told the audience the performance was canceled. In the days after, says Rohrbacher, her son couldn't forget the scene: "He keeps saying, 'You said it wasn't real, Mummy.'"

There are few realities more painfully concrete than an angry 600-lb. tiger. Horn had worked with Montecore for more than five years, raising him at the Jungle Palace, his nearby nature compound and home. (Fischbacher, then 63, lives apart in a gated community.) And he was wary of the dangers, said his friend, former *Lifestyles of the Rich and Famous* host Robin Leach: "There's a mantra that Roy always repeated: 'Never turn your back on these animals.'

Every night he realized he took his life in his hands."

Backstage, Horn was bleeding profusely from puncture wounds to his neck. He managed to gasp, "Don't shoot [the tiger]." Some crew members formed a circle and prayed; others used their fingers to stanch the bleeding while awaiting the medics.

By the time Horn arrived at University Medical Center's trauma unit seven minutes later, "he was still talking, still breathing," said Robert Leinbach, public information officer for the Clark County Fire Department. "We tried to get a tube down his throat, and he fought it, which is good; it means he didn't need it. He could breathe on his own. He talked about his throat hurting." While famous friends called the hospital—Liz Taylor, Michael Jackson, Arnold Schwarzenegger and even, reportedly, Mick Jagger—Horn's condition was too fragile to allow anyone by his bedside other than an intimate inner circle of friends and family.

The next day, Horn sent a heartening message to the shell-shocked friends holding vigil in his hospital room. He did it in silence. "I went over to the bed and said, 'Roy, can you hear me?'" says Wynn. "'I'm holding your hand. If you can hear me, squeeze.' And he did. I said, 'Okay, one squeeze is yes and two squeezes is no.' I told Roy, 'Your body took a terrific shock. You lost a lot of blood. The doctors have had to do surgeries on you. Can you handle this?' And Roy squeezed my hand once for yes."

Still, that night, the show's producer assembled the staff and told them they would have to clean out their lockers for the indefinite future. "They made a pact a long time ago," said Leach, "that if either was ill, incapacitated or unable to work, the other doesn't go on without him. There is no Siegfried and Roy without Roy."

In the days that followed, hun-

Still a hit after 13 years, the Siegfried and Roy extravaganza at the Mirage in Las Vegas grossed $1 million a week. The stage has been used just for a single fund-raiser since the attack.

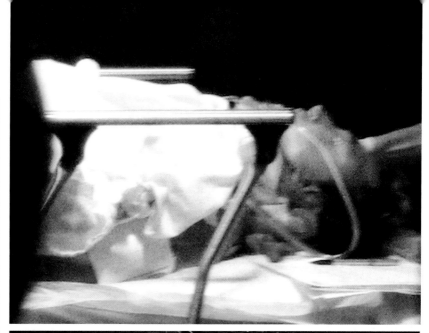

dreds of fans gathered outside the hospital to pray. Fischbacher, Roy's partner of nearly 45 years, was at his bedside nearly around the clock, kept company by a stream of friends and colleagues. Although Wynn describes him as "devastated" during the first few days—"If you looked at his face, you got it; it was frightening"—Siegfried soon began to take charge of the situation. "Siegfried has unconditional faith," says Bernie Yuman, the duo's manager.

Horn was in shock and had lost so much blood that at one point his heart stopped. He was revived, but terrible damage was also done by a severe stroke he suffered after the attack. To relieve the swelling in his brain, doctors removed a section of his skull, implanting it temporarily in his abdomen, where it would not be contaminated by outside exposure. By Christmas the swelling had gone down enough for the bone plate to be replaced in the skull. Horn had also been weaned from a respirator and regained some sight in his left eye.

Only after months of physical therapy did Horn appear again in public. In mid-2005, he entered a German clinic for an experimental treatment that uses stem cells from pig embryos to stimulate and repair damaged nerve cells. So far, Horn still has limited use of his left side.

When he did reemerge, Horn finally spoke of the attack. "Montecore," he insisted, "saved my life." He claimed that even onstage he began to experience dizzy spells or minor strokes. When he fell, Montecore, Horn said, recognized that he was in danger and dragged him to a safer place where he could get help. Doctors are not as certain of that scenario, though wildlife experts have noted that if a white tiger wanted to kill a man, it could do so easily.

As for their show, after 13 years, it folded. Montecore still lives at the Mirage's Secret Garden zoo, in an area off limits to the public.

"Thank God I'm a cat with nine lives," said Horn (top, after surgery the night of the attack, and, above right, favoring his partially paralyzed left side in a stroll with Fischbacher in October of 2005). "I'm on my ninth life now, so I still have a little bit more to do." The duo have considered a return someday to the stage.

JESSICA: THE BABY IN THE WELL

In 1987 a toddler fell down a 30-foot hole—and her fate became a national obsession

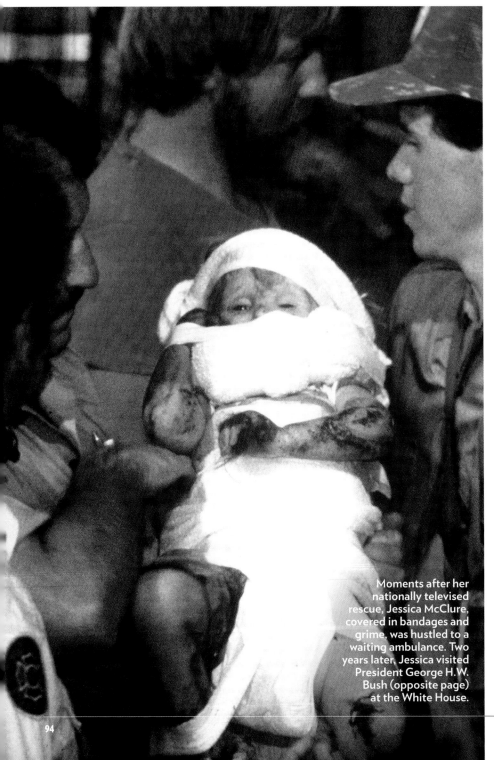

Moments after her nationally televised rescue, Jessica McClure, covered in bandages and grime, was hustled to a waiting ambulance. Two years later, Jessica visited President George H.W. Bush (opposite page) at the White House.

CISSY McCLURE, 18, had stepped away for just a moment when she heard the children screaming. Racing back into the yard where 18-month-old Jessica had been playing with four other toddlers, Cissy found no trace of her daughter. Then she saw the narrow mouth of the abandoned well. Usually it was covered by a heavy rock or flower pot. But on the morning of Oct. 14, 1987, the hole was open and Cissy's daughter Jessica had fallen in. "I didn't know what to do," Cissy said. "I just ran in and called the police. They were there within three minutes, but it felt like a lifetime."

BOBBIE JO HALL, 32, a Midland, Texas, police officer: The mother met us at the front door of the house. She yelled, "She's here in back! She fell down right here!" Then she said, "I can't let my baby die! I've got to get her out!" I went over and looked down the hole, but I couldn't see anything. I called the baby's name three or four times and didn't hear anything. Finally I got a cry in response. We didn't know how deep she was until we lowered a tape hooked to a flashlight into the hole.

A rescue crew was quickly assembled. The first strategy was to use a backhoe to dig next to the shaft until the girl could be freed. But the machine hit solid rock about three feet down; Jessica was nearly 30 feet below the surface.

ANDY GLASSCOCK, 36, detective: We began to shout down the well, and Jessica responded with whimpers. After listening to her for so long, I could tell her moods. At one point she was singing. At another point, when a jackhammer started up, she didn't say any words but used kind of a huffy little voice. You could tell it was an angry voice. Eighty percent of the time she was either crying or making some kind of noise we could hear. I'll never forget her singing "Winnie-the-Pooh." We'd say, "How does a kitten go?" And she'd respond.

DAVID LILLY, 51, *with the U.S. Mine Safety and Health Administration, was brought in from New Mexico to direct the rescue. He found local crews drilling a hole parallel to the well shaft; they intended to break into the shaft where Jessica was stuck. Fearing that approach would bring the walls down on top of her, he changed the angle to break into the shaft below her.*

LILLY: We were going at about an inch an hour. It was terribly hard rock, and it was slow going because you had to lie down on your stomach holding a 45-lb. jackhammer in front of you. But I've never seen more dedicated people. We actually had to force some of the men to quit and leave because they were about to drop. One guy was lying on the ground throwing his guts out. Another dropped from exhaustion, and we had to carry him out. It was a sight to see.

When I finally broke through into the shaft under where the girl was, I reached in and felt her foot and leg. When I had done that and heard her start crying, from that point on every time we'd go down and work for a little while, we'd have to stop because all the men, including myself, were getting so upset at hearing that baby cry. All the men, the chippers and drillers, would start bawling.

She'd been slipping on us. She was dehydrating, so I guess as she got smaller she slipped further down. That had me worried. I drilled straight across the well about two feet under her and inserted a metal rod to stop her descent. Then I inserted an industrial-strength bal-

loon into the well under her to protect her from the dust and noise.

Once the excavation crew cleared an opening a few feet below Jessica, paramedics were called to get her out safely.

ROBERT O'DONNELL, 30, para-medic: We didn't know how she went into the well. If it was head-first, she could have neck and spine damage, and any movement could have snapped the cord and we'd be bringing up a dead baby. On Friday at about 1 p.m. they said they were ready for us. I wasn't scared, but I was real apprehensive—I was going 29 feet down inside a black hole. I was wearing a mining light and a harness connected to a cable, and they lowered me slowly.

Once he reached the bottom of the new shaft, he inched along a horizontal passageway to a position below Jessica.

O'DONNELL: When I looked up, I saw Jessica's left foot dangling. Her parents had told us her nickname was Juicy, and that's what I called her. I said, "Move your foot for me, Juicy," and she'd do it. She'd whine once in a while, but she wouldn't talk words. I wanted to see what kind of physical condition she was in. I took her left leg and pressed up on it, and she didn't act like she was in pain.

Given the narrowness of the tunnel, O'Donnell couldn't pull Jessica out safely. Leaving her behind, he went up to the surface and asked the excavation crew to widen the open-

ings so he could get closer to Jessica, who was stuck with one leg above her and the other below. At about 6 o'clock, O'Donnell went back in.

O'DONNELL: We had talked about what we'd have to do this time, because we were going on 50 hours and the pressure to get Jessica out had mounted to a high intensity. We had gotten to the point where if we had to get physical to pull her out, we were not going to worry about broken legs, broken arms, nothing—as long as we kept her back, neck and head intact. The rest could be fixed. Whatever broke, broke.

They had given me two or three more inches height-wise in the tunnel, but they didn't get me any closer to her. I lined the walls of the shaft with K-Y jelly and started pulling. She didn't like it at all. She had blue baby pants with snaps, and I got my hands wrapped in them pretty good and just kept pulling. She kept yelling, screaming, crying. One time she cut loose a big "No!" I kept calling her Juicy and telling her to calm down, but every time I pulled she tensed up real hard. So I'd keep a snug grip, and just when she'd relax, I'd yank even harder. Over and over I did this.

Finally I noticed I had moved her two inches, then three inches. Then I got her into the K-Y jelly, and she started moving even better. I pulled again and she came down. She was facing me, both arms beside her head. I said, "You're out, Juicy." I didn't have to tell her to calm down, because she was totally calm already. She wasn't moving, nothing. She was just blinking her eyes, looking around.

Jessica was strapped to a board and slowly raised by cable to the surface, where an ambulance rushed her to the hospital.

HALL: The route we took to the hospital—I was behind the ambulance—the streets were lined with people, and they were all cheering, and the church bells were all ringing. It was the greatest thing I've ever seen.

HEAVEN'S GATE

Despondent, Kenneth Baldwin leaped off the Golden Gate Bridge. His first thought? 'Oh my God, this was a bad idea.' Miraculously, he lived

"My life did flash before me," Baldwin (in 1987) said later. "I thought I really blew it."

ONE OF THE MOST BEAUTIFUL SUSPENSION BRIDGES IN THE WORLD, SAN FRANCISCO'S *Golden Gate Bridge is also famous for another reason: suicide. In the past 68 years an estimated 1,300 people are thought to have jumped from the bridge—giving it the dubious reputation as perhaps the world's leading venue for ending it all. Only 26 people are known to have taken the 249-foot plunge and lived. Kenneth Baldwin is one of them. On the morning of Aug. 21, 1985, the Tracy, Calif., computer draftsman, then 28, told his wife, Ellen, that he planned to work overtime that night and would be unable to pick up their daughter Catherine, 3, from the babysitter.*

Cherishing a life that once seemed bleak, Baldwin savors his time with Ellen and Catherine (in 1987).

I had been thinking about suicide for some time. But I don't really know why, on that day, I decided to jump from the bridge. I had been depressed about work for months. I was afraid I was going to be fired. Ellen had supported the family for two years while I went to school to learn drafting. She had really sacrificed for me, and I was going to let her down. I felt incredible pressure. In school I had gotten good grades, but out in the real world I felt I couldn't cut it. Or worse, that my family couldn't depend on me. I really believed that killing myself would be an act of love for my family. I imagined Ellen marrying someone who was very responsible, a man who could always make the mortgage payments. But I have to admit that part of my desire to die was selfish. I was in such pain, such anguish, I wanted it to stop. I wanted to escape.

Baldwin chose the Golden Gate because, he said, "it wasn't messy," like some other forms of suicide.

I heard the current in the bay was so strong the bodies were often swept out to sea and sometimes never found. I found that reassuring. I didn't want my family going through a funeral. I just wanted them to forget me, to let me go.

After leaving home that day, Baldwin made the 90-minute drive

to the Golden Gate. But once he got out of his car and stood on the bridge, he had second thoughts.

I kept thinking of my wife and daughter. I loved them deeply. And I wondered what it would feel like to hit the water. I realized it might hurt. I didn't want to fall on top of a boat. I didn't want anyone standing near me when I jumped. I felt I had been treated badly, and I wanted to tell the world how I felt. No one really noticed me. Well, they were going to notice me now. Suddenly, there were many things to consider.

Baldwin counted to 10 but couldn't jump. When he reached 10 the second time, he glanced briefly across the bay at the city of San Francisco and went over the side.

I remember my hands leaving the railing, the sensation of falling. I instantly realized I had made a mistake. I can't tell you how frightening that was. I didn't want to die. Yet here I was heading for certain death. There was nothing I could do about it. I was falling feetfirst with my legs pulled under me a little. Before I hit, I blacked out— from fear, I guess.

After falling for three seconds, Baldwin smashed into the water at 75 mph. The impact subjected parts of his body to pressures of 15,000 pounds per square inch, a power often likened to that of a speeding car

hitting a brick wall. Jumpers generally suffer massive internal injuries, but Baldwin's buttocks and thighs absorbed the worst of the shock. He came to underwater, wondering briefly whether he was alive or dead.

When I surfaced I instinctively started swimming and yelling for help. I remember shouting, "Help me! Help me!" God, I was happy to be alive.

Rescued by the Coast Guard, Baldwin arrived at Letterman Army Medical Center fully conscious, apologetic and suffering slightly from exposure; he had a bruised lung and a cracked rib.

The damage to his marriage was more severe. When Ellen was first told her husband had leaped from the bridge, she laughed, believing it was a joke. Then she went into shock. "I didn't know what to think," she told PEOPLE. *"Generally, when you've been married for a while, you think you know your partner. Kenny always comes across as a fun-loving, outgoing guy. And I thought we were the perfect family. His suicide attempt took me completely by surprise. I knew he was unhappy about work. But who is so unhappy that they would kill themselves?"*

Ellen felt confused, guilty, angry. At one point she considered leaving Ken. Therapy helped keep the two of them together. Twenty years later, they are still married. Now 48, Ken teaches drafting at a vocational high school near Stockton. Ellen, also 48, is a graphic artist, and daughter Catherine, 23, is studying to become a teacher.

I've learned to lean on my wife when I need help. I still feel anxious often, but now I talk it out and I realize this isn't permanent, it's just feeling bad. Life got better right away [after the jump]. Everybody's got their rocky roads and their bad days, and I still do too. But I feel I have more options now.

Ever since I landed in the water, I've felt that I wanted to live, and nothing has taken that away.

BURIED IN BEANS

Jim Rolland climbed into a silo to make a repair, and quickly found himself sinking in soybeans

"He couldn't have done anything better that day," a grateful Rolland (right, knee-deep in beans) said of Ryan Jensen, the pal who helped save him.

THINGS WERE GOING JUST FINE March 23, 2004, when the flow of soybeans cascading down from a 75-ft.-high bin into a waiting railcar below suddenly shut down. Frustrated, Jim Rolland, 47, climbed some stairs alongside the bin to a portal, then squeezed inside on top of the mountain of stuck beans. "I thought I could fix it," he said later, "and then get out."

As he was getting started, the beans shifted and Rolland sank like a stone up to his chin. "It was like getting caught in an avalanche," says Rolland, who couldn't move anything but his toes and could barely breathe. "I could

feel the beans settling tighter around me, like quicksand." With the beans stored at a bone-chilling 40°, he also risked suffering hypothermia.

Hearing his friend's cries, coworker Ryan Jensen, 23, yelled for someone to phone 911, then scampered into the bin through the same portal Rolland had used, only to find the top half of his buddy's head sticking out of the beans. "What can I do?" Jensen asked. "You could pray," Rolland said. "I am," said Jensen. He also took action. Lying flat on his belly to spread his weight and avoid sinking in himself, Jensen gingerly made his way to Rolland. "I tried to

keep him calm," says Jensen. "I knew that meant keeping him alive."

While rescue workers gathered outside the Osage, Iowa, silo, Jensen stayed with Rolland for nearly four hours, keeping his air passages clear by sweeping beans away from his face. Finally, using a special vacuum, rescuers sucked the beans from around Rolland and pulled him out with ropes and a stretcher. He was then airlifted to a Rochester, Minn., hospital, where he was declared okay. "If Ryan hadn't jumped in," said Osage volunteer fire department chief Kurt Angell, "we probably would've been recovering a body."

CHAPTER 6

FIGHTING BACK

MAKING THE CHOICE TO BATTLE THE BAD GUYS

BRAVER THAN THEY KNEW

Kidnapped at gunpoint, two California teenagers teamed up, fought back and lived

Jacque Marris's friends cele-
brated her rescue. "When the
announcement came that the
girls had been found, this community went wild," said Dr. Billy
Pricer, chaplain for the L.A.
County Sheriff's Department.

"I knew that I wasn't alone in this," said a thankful Jacque Marris (back-to-back with co-captive Tamara Brooks and, from left, Jacque's grandmother Theresa Monares, mother, Nadine Dyer, and Tamara's mother, Sharon Brooks).

OUT AROUND THE EDGE *of the Mojave Desert, an hour or so north of Los Angeles, things can get pretty slow. To break the monotony, teens from the neighboring towns of Lancaster and Palmdale often drive up to Quartz Hill. There, overlooking Antelope Valley, they park— some for a romantic evening, some just to listen to music and gaze at the stars. Tamara Brooks, a 16-year-old honors student and track star from Antelope Valley High, was sitting with Eric Brown, 18, in his white Ford Bronco in the early hours of Thur., Aug. 1, 2002, when a stranger emerged from the darkness.*

BROOKS: When he came up to the window, at first I thought it was the police and we were in trouble. Then I saw the gun. He said, "Give me all your money." I didn't even have a purse. I was terrified. I was shaking. I was trying to appear calm but I had the biggest lump in my throat. He told Eric to get out. Eric kept saying, "I don't want to die." I was praying, "Please let me live. I want to live to see my family."

The man led Brown away, bound him with duct tape, then returned, saying at first he just wanted the SUV. Then, apparently, he changed his mind and taped her arm to the car door. At the time, Brooks had no idea that the thug was Roy Ratliff, 37, a career criminal who had previous burglary and drug convictions and was wanted for rape. An hour later, having left Brooks in the SUV, Ratliff sneaked up on another unsuspecting couple, Jacque Marris, 17, a cheerleader from nearby Highland High, and her friend Frank Melero, 19, who was training to become an EMT.

MELERO: All of the sudden he was at my door. He stuck the gun in my face and told me to throw out my wallet. He took about $60 and seemed really mad. He wanted some rope. I had some in the back of the truck. He kept the gun in my back when I got out of the car and went to get it. He

was talking all tough, like a mobster. He was calling me "dude" and "bro." He asked me my name and would say, "You think you're a tough guy, Frank?" Back in the truck he began hitting me in the face. I could smell the booze.

Just as Ratliff fastened Melero's hands and legs with tape, a state Water and Power worker pulled up, unaware of what was happening, and began walking around.

MELERO: [Ratliff] was standing at my window. He said, "Don't move or I'll kill you."

MARRIS: I told Frank how scared I was, and he said God would take care of us. His hands were tied together and mine were still free. So I held his hands and we prayed. Then the guy took me out of the car. I was so scared.

Ratliff bundled Marris into the Bronco with Brooks and sped away. Minutes later, Melero freed himself and used a cell phone to call his

mother, Carmen, who dialed 911. Police arrived and found Brown, who gave then a description of his Bronco. Meanwhile, Marris and Brooks did their best to keep up their spirits.

MARRIS: We knew how worried our parents, family and friends would be; we felt awful. I started to softly sing "Blessed" and stroke Tamara's leg and arms. I always sing when I'm mad or in trouble. It's a comfort.

BROOKS: It was like my mom singing a lullaby to me.

MARRIS: At one point he stopped the car just off the highway and left the passenger door ajar. I could see cars coming by and I could kind of figure out when I could jump out and flag someone down. Maybe I could get away, but I didn't know what would happen to Tamara. I couldn't leave her behind. We were loosely tied and had duct tape over our mouths. We began to communicate by drawing letters on each other's hands. The first thing we wrote was "What shall we do?"

Brooks looked around for a knife she knew Brown kept in the car, thinking maybe she and Marris could overpower Ratliff. Finally, they found it, plus a bottle they thought they could use as a weapon. When Ratliff pulled over again and parked, they tore at him. Marris lashed out with the knife, Brooks bashed him in the face with the bottle, and they shoved him out the door and locked it. They had done some damage—but not enough.

MARRIS: He was yelling, "Open the door or I'll kill you!" We were yelling back at him. I was saying, "Don't you believe in Jesus? Isn't there going to be anyone who will be upset if you die?" He told us that no one cared about him. Then he fired a warning shot over the car. We knew we had to let him in. He told us he'd have to shoot one of us because he couldn't handle us both.

Authorities had issued a public alert about the kidnapping and received a tip around 11:30 a.m. Someone had seen the Bronco speeding down a remote highway about 100 miles north of Quartz Hill. Then a county employee caught a glimpse of the SUV heading down a dirt track. She alerted authorities, and within minutes a helicopter and police cars appeared. Two deputies jumped out of their car and ordered Ratliff to surrender. Instead he raised his gun.

MARRIS: All of the sudden I saw the police, and they were shooting at him. He climbed over the seat and was right beside me. He had his head on my shoulder. I was waving to the shooter to tell him that we were in there too.

BROOKS: I saw bullets go into his body.

MARRIS: When the cops first came up, he yelled, "I have the girls," like he was using us as a hostage. But when he yelled the last time, he looked me in the eye with such despair. It was like he was telling the cops, Don't shoot the girls. In a crazy way, I think he was protecting us.

After the girls were hustled out of the car, the wounded Ratliff managed to raise his gun one more time. A deputy took aim and fired, hitting Ratliff in the head and killing him.

The girls kept in touch after that night, bound by the horror they had shared—and survived.

MARRIS: We were really there for each other.

BROOKS: When we knew we were safe, it was like my soul soaring. The dictionary has no words for this feeling. You are every minute thankful to be alive.

> " He fired a warning shot over the car. We knew we had to let him in. He told us he'd have to shoot one of us because he couldn't handle us both"

The body of Roy Ratliff (above) is carried away by authorities (left).

"We were just thinking about the children and how we could get them safe," said Bentzel (her hands still wrapped in bandages after fighting off William Stankewicz, opposite page).

THE KILLER AND THE KIDS

A madman with a machete attacked her kindergarten; the principal leapt on his back

NORINA BENTZEL, the principal of North Hopewell-Winterstown Elementary School in Red Lion, Pa., was just getting off the phone when she saw a stranger enter the school. Thinking he might be one of her student's grandfathers, she hung up and walked out to greet him. "I asked if there was something I could do," she says. In response, the man whipped out a long black object and began swinging. Before Bentzel could respond, the man had bruised her shoulder and slashed her right hand.

"It felt like a piece of wood," says Bentzel, 42. "I didn't know it was a machete."

When the stranger took a swipe at her stomach, Bentzel barely managed to jump away. "Then he turned and ran back down the hallway," she recalls. "I yelled out, 'Call 911! Lockdown!'" She ran to her office and pressed an alarm button that signaled teachers to lock their doors, but she was too late to stop the slasher from bursting into a kindergarten classroom filled with 23 students.

"The kids were screaming," says teacher Linda Collier, 53. The stranger came in swinging and sliced one child's hand and another's ponytail before Collier distracted him. "I hollered, 'What do you think you're doing? Stop hitting them!'" says Collier. Turning on her, the stranger sliced a gash in her hand.

The children bolted from the room toward the principal's office with the man in hot pursuit. Bentzel herded them inside, then found herself face-to-face with the assailant, who began raining down blows, fracturing her left forearm and nearly severing her pinkie. Collier and school nurse Denise Zellers came up from behind. When the man turned, Bentzel saw that it might be her only chance to stop him and leapt on his back. "I yelled, 'Help me get him down!'" she says.

"He dropped the machete, and I remember feeling the life draining from him. He slumped over a desk. I said, 'Calm down, it's over.'"

The stranger said, "Arlen Specter made me do this." "What?" Bentzel said in disbelief.

When paramedics and police arrived 10 minutes later, they found Bentzel semiconscious from loss of blood. After treatment in a nearby hospital, she had her left pinkie and ring finger reattached at the Curtis National Hand Center in Baltimore.

On Sept. 26, 2001, nearly eight months after the assault, William Stankewicz, 56, pleaded guilty to two counts of attempted murder and 16 counts of aggravated assault. He was sentenced to 132 to 264 years in prison. A former schoolteacher with a history of mental problems, he had been divorced in 1995 by his mail-order bride from Kazakhstan. He wanted her deported and served two years in prison for making death threats against federal officials who had declined to take action.

Seeking revenge against his ex-wife, he traveled to Red Lion—where the couple had once lived—from his home in Tennessee. When he couldn't find her, he struck out at the school her two children had attended. As for Senator Specter (R-Pa.), his alleged involvement was merely a product of Stankewicz's delusions.

Colleagues weren't surprised by Bentzel's heroics. Said her secretary, Susan Capp: "I liken it to a mother bear protecting her young."

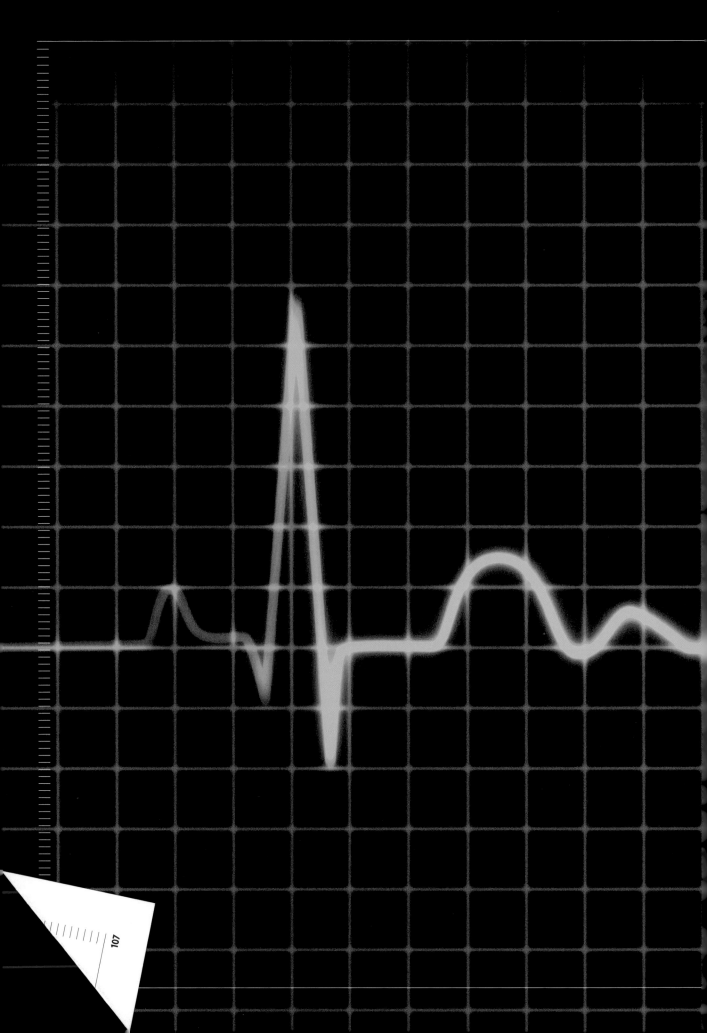

CHAPTER 7

MEDICAL MIRACLES

SOMETIMES SCIENCE CAN DO WONDERS

"Sometimes we worry about how we'll manage," Chris said of the financial strains on himself and Jennifer (with Courtney in 2004), "but then it all generally steers itself around."

THE ONE-POUND WONDER

In her perilous first year of life, micropreemie Courtney Jackson defied the odds

UP TO *80 percent of babies born before the 24th week of pregnancy do not survive. Many that do eventually suffer severe physical handicaps including cerebral palsy and blindness.*

In 2001, Jennifer Jackson of Bloomfield, Iowa, gave birth to daughter Courtney just 23 weeks into her pregnancy, below the six-month threshold considered necessary for survival.

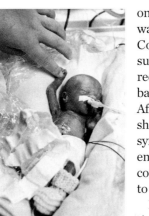

On the evening of June 18, Jennifer, then 25 and pregnant with her first child, called her obstetrician to report a splitting headache and vomiting. Suddenly she began moaning. She was having a seizure—the first of four she would endure before arriving at a medical center 95 miles away.

Stricken with eclampsia, a little-understood condition that causes a pregnant woman's blood pressure to soar—and can kill her unborn child—Jennifer was unconscious when her husband, Chris, 26, allowed doctors to quickly induce birth.

Courtney began life weighing only 460 grams, a fraction over 1 lb. Eleven inches long, she had a total of eight teaspoons of blood and a heart the size of an acorn. Doctors gave her parents a grim prognosis: As a so-called micropreemie—the smallest of all premature babies—Courtney had a 50 percent chance of survival.

She also seemed to have a fierce determination to live. When doctors inserted a tiny breathing tube, "Courtney grabbed at it and hit our hands while we were working," one doctor recalled. "She just wanted to get it out of her way." Courtney breezed through surgery a month later to correct a defect in her heart and battled chronic lung problems. After four months of IV feeding, she began tasting milk from a syringe. Soon she was strong enough to take a bottle. "You could tell she was going to fight to come home," said Chris.

Despite the dark predictions, Courtney was living at home at 5 months old—albeit tethered to an oxygen tank, which Jennifer hauled along as she took Courtney to her job at a nearby daycare center.

Against all odds, Courtney thrived. By her third birthday in 2004 she weighed 28 lbs., within the normal range. Physically active, she was intellectually alert and emotionally unscathed, said her doctors. "We can't make every one of these premature babies survive," said Dr. John Widness, who led the neonatology team caring for Courtney in the first month of her life. "But when you see one like her do so spectacularly well, it's what you live for."

After celebrating her third birthday, Courtney was in the driveway of her family home, being pushed by her father on a new tricycle. "To think that three years ago we started off with this little, itty-bitty thing," said Chris, watching his daughter struggle to work the pedals. "Now it won't be long before she learns to ride it herself."

THE GREATEST COMEBACK

KO'd by cancer, written off as an athlete, Lance Armstrong fought back to win the world's toughest race seven times

"I never thought I'd get cancer," said Armstrong (left, in the 1999 Tour de France and, above, in July 2005 with his then-fiancée, singer Sheryl Crow). "But young, strong men should realize this can happen."

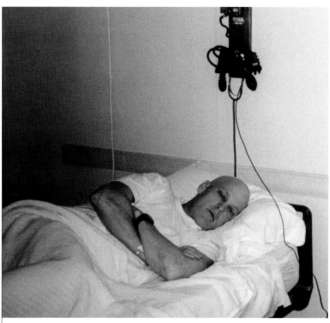

"With my fitness level, my drive and my desire, I'm not going to lose," vowed a determined Armstrong (undergoing treatment in the fall of 1996). "I can't lose."

FOR LANCE ARMSTRONG, it had been a golden summer. In May 1996 the cyclist had won the 12-day, 1,200-mile Tour DuPont—then America's most prestigious bicycle race—for the second year in a row. He'd been one of America's top cyclists at the Summer Olympics, and that August placed fourth in the Grand Prix of Switzerland. Better still, he had just begun to collect the perks showered on elite athletes: a $2 million contract to compete for France's Team Cofidis and a Nike endorsement deal. "Twenty-five and entering the peak of my career," he said. "I felt bulletproof."

He wasn't. The first warning came in July, when bronchitis forced the normally fit young man to drop out of the Tour de France. Then, even as he notched 6th- and 12th-place finishes at the Olympics, racing left him more fatigued than usual. In late September he coughed up blood, and on Sept. 28 he felt a pain in his right testicle. Until then, long accustomed to the discomforts of pushing a bike seven hours a day, Armstrong had shrugged off the symptoms. "You have to perform with pain as an athlete," he said.

Finally, in October, limping with pain, he went to a doctor. The diagnosis: testicular cancer. Worse, the disease had spread to his lungs, brain and abdomen. Doctors gave him a 40 percent chance of survival. "I was in shock," he recalled. "I put my head down on the doctor's desk and thought about it for a couple of minutes. But there was no point denying it, so I looked up and said, 'Let's get started. Let's kill this stuff.'"

Armstrong had his cancerous testicle removed the next morning and, after recuperating, reported for his first session of chemotherapy. A sec-ond surgery removed two lesions from his brain. On the advice of a nutritionist, he also radically altered his diet, giving up red meat, dairy products—even his beloved coffee. Still, the chemotherapy dragged him down, and by the end of his first week he found himself taking two-hour naps every afternoon, even after sleeping 10 hours at night.

That was unusual for Armstrong, said his mother, Linda Armstrong Kelly, a secretary who raised him as a single mother in Plano, Texas. "He was high-energy all the time," she recalled. Pointing him toward sports in fifth grade, she watched him become a disciplined distance runner who, at 13, discovered competitive cycling. Invited to international races while still in high school, Armstrong spent weeks in Europe racing against the world's best.

His effort paid off. U.S. Amateur champ at 20, Armstrong first represented the U.S. at the '92 Olympics, then turned pro in 1993, when he took six titles for the Motorola team, winning the World Championships, the U.S. Nationals and one of the 20 stages of the Tour de France.

Then cancer hit, and his quick rise came to a sudden halt. Even when doctors declared in 1997 that his cancer was gone and there was only a marginal chance it would recur, many wondered whether he could ever again be competitive.

Two years later, in the 21-day, 2,287-mile 1999 Tour de France, he handed the sporting world his answer. Then 27, Armstrong finished more than seven minutes ahead of his nearest competitor. "After I got sick," he said, "the mentality in cycling was 'He's finished, done, history.'" His victory over 180 of the world's best riders, he added, "sends a message that cancer is not a death sentence. . . . I'm stronger physically now than I was before."

He was just getting started. In the summer of 2005, Armstrong, the greatest athlete in one of the world's most demanding sports, won a record seventh consecutive Tour de France. Announcing his retirement, he said he would devote more time to, among other things, the foundation he created to help raise cancer awareness.

After Armstrong won his last title, Linda summed up her son's success: "Every year he won the Tour de France was a miracle. That he's this wonderful 33-year-old man with three beautiful children is a miracle. To have accomplished something that no one else has ever accomplished and continue to give back to cancer patients—that is the man that he is. He is a proud American."

"When I see Marissa-Eve," said Anissa (right, with her sister and mother in 1994), "she's like a light that turns on inside me."

BORN TO SAVE A LIFE

Anissa Ayala is alive because her little sister exists

SIXTEEN YEARS OLD and unable to find a matching bone-marrow donor, Anissa Ayala faced certain death from leukemia. Then her parents, Mary, then 41, and Abe, 44, had an amazing, risky idea: They would try to create a donor by having another child. Both parents were aware that there was no guarantee that the baby's marrow would match Anissa's. (Neither their own nor their 18-year-old son Airon's was suitable.)

What the Walnut, Calif., family weren't prepared for was the furor their decision would ignite. Medical ethicists decried the plan. The family was deluged with angry letters and phone calls. Still, Mary and Abe were not going to sit by and watch their daughter die. "My parents did the only thing they could do," said Anissa. "I look on them as heroes."

Their determination paid off. Even before Marissa-Eve was born on April 4, 1990, amniocentesis and tissue-typing tests revealed that her marrow was a match. Fourteen months later, with Marissa-Eve under anesthesia, the transfer procedure was performed. As the baby grew into a healthy child, the public debate died down—and the Ayalas rejoiced. "We knew it was the right thing to do," said Abe. "We thought we were going to lose a daughter, and now we have two."

CHAPTER 8

WORLD OF WAR

SCENES FROM A VIOLENT WORLD

A FRIENDSHIP TESTED BY FIRE

Eric Alva lost his leg to an Iraqi land mine. Brian Alaniz rushed to help and lost his leg too. In the end, the pain of recovery was no match for the bond they forged

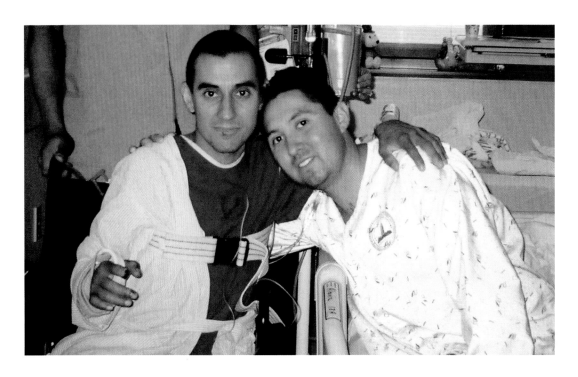

WHEN THE 3RD BATTALION, *7th Marines, got the call in March 2003 to cross the border into Iraq, Staff Sgt. Eric Alva, 32, and Brian Alaniz, 28, a medic, were nervous, but ready to roll. Two Texans a world away from home, they had met during training in Kuwait that winter and become good friends.*

ALANIZ: On March 21 our convoy was headed toward Basra. It was about 11 a.m. when we stopped. The area was sort of rural—sand and desert. Everyone got out to stretch their legs.
ALVA: We were told to be careful where we walked. So we were all looking at the ground. It was when I lifted my eyes for just a couple of seconds that I stepped on the land mine. Then it was mass chaos;

"It's almost as if we were meant to be friends," Alaniz said of his connection to Alva (left in both photos, at the hospital in Bethesda, Md., and at Alaniz's parents' home).

everyone was running around and shouting. It's weird, but one of my first thoughts was about two new guys in my unit. They were only 18 and 19, and all I could think was how scared they must be seeing all the blood, hearing all the screaming and realizing this was all for real—we were really in a war. Then I felt the medics cut the laces off my left boot. They never touched my right leg, which tells me I'd probably lost it by then. But I was too scared to look.

He had no idea that Alaniz was among the medics who rushed to his aid—nor did Alaniz know Alva was the injured one.

ALANIZ: I was kneeling down, putting together a suction device, when the second land mine went off right underneath me. I'd been on top of it all along, but it didn't detonate until I shifted my weight. I felt like I was on fire from midthigh down. Everything seemed in slow motion. No one came to help me at first. They'd been told to freeze, in case there were other land mines. Finally they picked me up on a stretcher and put me in an ambulance. I kept asking, "How bad is it?" They kept telling me, "You're going to be just fine," but they wouldn't meet my eyes—so I knew I wasn't all right.

Both men were taken by helicopter to Kuwait City.

ALANIZ: On the chopper I really started to feel the pain. My hand was dangling off the stretcher, and I could feel someone grab it. I gripped that hand for the whole flight. Only later did I find out it was Eric's.

Alva's right arm was blown open, his left leg was broken, and he was riddled with shrapnel. In a hospital tent near Kuwait City he was anesthetized. Awakening hours later, he saw his leg had been amputated, then fell back to sleep. The next morning Alaniz, who still had both

Nine months after they were wounded, Alaniz (above left) and Alva went skiing. President Bush paid a visit to Alaniz while he was still recovering (far right).

legs, woke up in the shock-trauma tent to find Alva sleeping in the bed next to his.

ALANIZ: I looked over at him on that cot, and I prayed that he'd be okay. The next day, I was taken to a field hospital. I was fading in and out from the morphine, but I remember the doctor telling me the bones in my leg were too shattered to repair and that they'd have to amputate. It all began to dawn on me; I started thinking about my wife, wondering if she'd even want to stay married to me.

Alva finally learned that Alaniz had gone to his aid—and had also lost a leg.

ALVA: The drugs were starting to wear off, and everything hit me; losing my leg, causing Brian to lose his leg. I cried myself to sleep. When I woke up, I was being wheeled to an airplane to take me to the military hospital in Landstuhl, Germany. Brian was on the same plane, but we didn't know it.

ALANIZ: In Germany they put us on a bus to the hospital. I felt nauseous. When the bus finally stopped, I started throwing up. A soldier below me said, "You better not throw up on me, man, or I'll kick your ass!" It turned out to be Eric—but I still didn't know it, and neither did he.

At Landstuhl, Alaniz visited Alva.

ALVA: We both started crying. The

first thing I told Brian was "Thank you" and "I'm sorry. If I hadn't gotten hurt, you wouldn't be here right now."

ALANIZ: I told him I was just doing my job. I held his hand and told him everything was going to be all right.

On March 30 they were flown to Bethesda National Naval Medical Center in Maryland, where they asked to be roommates. Alaniz's wife, Ammi, stayed in their room almost 24/7, sharing her husband's narrow hospital bed. Alva's mother, Lois, was also a constant presence.

ALVA: The blanket of love over us from both families helped our recovery so much. I kept getting bad news, though. On April 3 my right knee was amputated because there wasn't enough flesh left to close over the stump, meaning no room to connect a prosthesis. It seems I was crying all the time—everything hurt so bad. I remember telling my mom one night that I wished I'd died over there.

ALANIZ: I never felt I didn't want to live. But I worried a lot. How normal would I be? One night when neither of us could sleep, Eric told me his detailed account of the explosions, and I told him mine. It was painful to revisit, but in the long run it helped us. No one else in the world had shared that experience. We started joking a little after a while. It lightened the mood. We'd say things like, "Hey, we can get a two-for-one pedicure."

Dark times remained, especially for Alva, who recovered slowly.

ALANIZ: For a long time,

Eric didn't want to go to physical therapy. It was hard sometimes for him to see me, because within two weeks I went from a wheelchair to a walker to crutches. Eric would say, "Wow, I wish I was doing as good as you." I pushed and finally persuaded him to get up and try. I knew once he got out of bed, he'd start feeling better about himself.

He did, and in early December, both men accepted invitations to participate in the Disabled Sports USA Ski Spectacular in Breckenridge, Colo. Alva is an avid skier, but for Alaniz it was a first.

ALANIZ: I was using my prosthesis, so it was a little scary. I was afraid I'd be on my butt or on my face all the time. But I didn't fall as much as I thought I would! Now Eric, you couldn't get him off the mountain. He'd do seven or eight runs a day [on one leg].

ALVA: To be feeling snow blowing

around you, sun on your face, wind rushing past your ears! Nine months earlier, lying in a bed where I couldn't even roll over.

Alva went back to school to get a degree in social work. Alaniz left the service to study X-ray technology. The two men still get in touch regularly.

ALANIZ: We still compare our therapies and our up-and-down emotions in a way no one else can. I want to do anything I can to help him, and if that means just sitting there listening to him complain—which he does sometimes, then apologizes—that's what I do. He will always be a part of my life.

ALVA: It brightens me up every time I talk to him. I know he feels bad every time I have a setback, but he lifts me up with encouraging words. When it comes to stepping up to the plate with strength and support, he's No. 1—a true American hero.

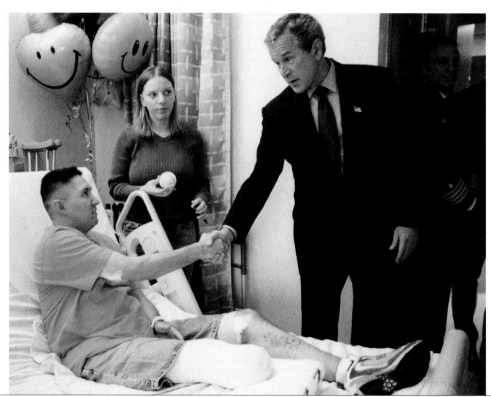

ENEMY TANKS ALL AROUND

"In the line of duty it says you gotta perform," said Bradish (left and far right, recovering in Tacoma, Wash.)

Frank Bradish went from the quiet hills of his native Idaho to the bloodstained desert of southern Iraq. Wounded and under fire, he found extraordinary courage

SHIPPED TO IRAQ *on Dec. 15, 1990, for the first Gulf War, Frank Bradish was assigned to a Bradley fighting vehicle with four others—a commander, gunner, driver and, like Bradish, another foot soldier. Their job: scout out the enemy. "I volunteered for the job," said Bradish, 20, a native of Pocatello, Idaho. "I like getting a close-up view of stuff." On Feb. 27, he did.*

It was about 8:30, and it was almost pitch black. I was in the back of the vehicle when the Iraqi tank came up. We shot at it and hit it. Then it shot at us. We heard *boom!* That was a blast from the Iraqi main gun hitting our tank. I felt our vehicle rock back really hard. . . . I thought, I gotta get out of here. So I went back, and I opened up the door, and I got shot.

There was probably another tank coming up behind us, because we got hit from the rear. Me and the other dismount were getting ready to go out. The same rounds that hit me hit him. A body won't stop a .50-cal. [machine gun] round. It went all the way through the vehicle's ramp, which is six inches thick with layered steel. It just blew right through that like nothing and then hit us. Then it went in the turret and hit the ready box, where the ammunition is stored, and set some rounds off. The bullets started blowing up, popping like firecrackers.

I felt the bullets hit me. It felt like someone was tugging on me. It didn't hurt on initial impact. I fell out [of the Bradley] and I started cussin'. I did a damage assessment on myself, and I said, "Well, my bones ain't broken, so I can still move around." Just the insides of my legs were screwed up. I felt down there and said, "Damn!" It was all numb down there and like Jell-O.

Bradish pulled the second dismount out of the Bradley. The man was critically wounded, and there was nothing Bradish could do to help him. Next he pulled out an M60 machine gun and radio, then sought out the other men.

I checked on the turret crew. I saw that the Bradley commander was dead. The gunner wasn't in the turret. I thought, Damn, where is he?

We stored our flares in a box on the top of the vehicle near the turret. It was dark, and so I got the whole box of 'em out. Then I climbed down. I was looking around and I heard moaning. It came from about 50 feet away. It was the gunner. He had gotten blown out of the turret and had a chest wound. So I dragged him back toward the tank.

The bullets from the Iraqis started coming really heavy on that side of the vehicle, so I couldn't check on the driver. I set up our defense and called the platoon leader on the radio. I said, "Hey, we're hit. We're down here and we're hit." [But radio network was so congested] I couldn't get through. I thought, I gotta let 'em know we're hit! And I thought of the flares.

There's like a sardine top on them that I could barely open when I had my hands intact, but now I got my finger shot off and a couple of others mangled, and I'm gonna have to do something else, so I held it with my teeth and pulled it off. Then I sent up the [flare] and the lieutenant saw it, 'cause I heard him say [on the radio], "Clear net!" I sent across our distress signal, and he said, "We'll be there in about five minutes."

About two minutes later our tank driver comes walking around from the other side of the vehicle, and he's all confused and he's saying, "What happened? What do I do?" He was kind of shell-shocked, but he didn't have any physical injury.

I told the driver to begin what we call "probing fire." It's a way of finding out where the enemy is. I said to him, "Go to the left flank and fire a shot every three or five minutes. Fire five or six rounds. When you see a muzzle flash, shoot a 40mm grenade at 'em and blow 'em up. If you see a whole bunch of muzzle flashes, I'll get over there with the M60 and we'll fire 'em up."

The platoon leader arrived in about 20 minutes. The medics came about five minutes later.

Bradish suffered wounds to both thighs and lost a testicle and part of a finger. After having surgery in Germany, he spent a month in an Army hospital in Tacoma, Wash., before heading home to Pocatello, where his family had a wicker basket full of letters written by people praising him for his heroism.

It doesn't mean that after you get shot that your duty's over. You just get slowed down.

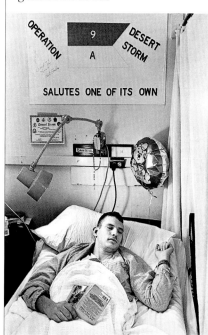

OPERATION DESERT STORM

9 A

SALUTES ONE OF ITS OWN

SEPT. 11, 2001

Survivors from the World Trade Center
and Pentagon recall the moments after impact

With 65 aboard, United Flight 175
crashed into the World Trade Center's
South Tower. "It was like the building
swallowed up the plane," said a witness.

SEPT. 11, 2001. The first plane—a 767, American Airlines Flight 11 from Boston—hit the North Tower of the World Trade Center at 8:46 a.m. Within 90 minutes planes had slammed into the South Tower, the Pentagon and a field in Shanksville, Pa. In all, 2,973 died, and America changed forever.

TINA HANSEN, 41, A PORT AUTHORITY MARKETING SUPERVISOR

When the first plane struck, Hansen, in a wheelchair and on the 68th floor of the World Trade Center, saw little reason to hope. "I didn't know how I was going to get out," she said.

Michael Benfante, 36, a communications company manager, spotted her. He and coworker John Cerqueira, 22, lifted Hansen and her lightweight wheelchair and began making their way down the stairwell. "We were a team," said Benfante. Along the way, "we tried to keep it light," adds Cerqueira. "I'd ask Tina, 'You all right, babe? You've got luxury service!'"

The mood darkened when they reached the fifth floor, which was pitch-black and flooded from the building's sprinklers. "It was like *The Poseidon Adventure*," said Benfante. "It was slippery, and I was moving stuff out of the way so we could push Tina. I wasn't going out unless she was with me."

When they reached the street, Hansen was placed in a waiting ambulance. Minutes later the tower began to collapse, and Benfante and Cerqueira—who narrowly escaped

the crashing debris—feared that the ambulance carrying Hansen might not have made it out. But a few days later Hansen spoke with her saviors. "Mike was really excited," said Hansen. "He said that hearing about me capped his day."

DAVID THEALL, 37, A PENTAGON PUBLIC AFFAIRS SPECIALIST

After the second plane hit the World Trade Center, Theall received a phone call from a close friend. Half kidding, she said, "'You know, the Pentagon is next. You better get out of there,'" recalled Theall.

Seconds later American Airlines Flight 77 crashed near Theall's office. "I watched the wall beside me crumple like a sheet of paper, and I was blown back 25 feet," he said. When he stopped moving, Theall was still clutching the phone. And already thinking about his next move. Climbing over a collapsed wall, Theall yelled for his dazed office mate Carl Mahnken, 39. "Cowboy, we've got to get out of here!" Theall urged.

As the air filled with smoke and fumes, Theall led Mahnken through the darkness. The two pulled themselves along with the help of dangling electrical wires and metal strips that once held up the ceil-

> On the 50th floor I wanted to rest, but a stranger, a guy named Doug, put his arm around me and said, 'If you can make it, let's keep going.' He kept telling me everything was going to be all right"

ing's tiles. "I knew instinctively where to go," said Theall.

Even after he and Mahnken ran into a concrete wall. Pulling back steel reinforcement to create an escape hole, the pair climbed into another office, where seven workers had been trapped before Theall led them out through the rubble. "I said, 'Man, you're like a bird dog—you're finding holes,'" Mahnken recalled. One of those holes led to "sunlight coming through the smoke," Theall said, and the group fled.

Having survived, Theall and Mahnken feel an extraordinary bond. "Carl and I have little in common," said Theall. "But now, just a look between us will mean something no one else can understand."

SILVION RAMSUNDAR, 31, AN INVESTMENT EXECUTIVE

He could still feel his legs. Based on that, said Ramsundar, "I knew I had a chance to make it." What he didn't

know was how badly he was injured.

On the 78th floor of the South Tower during the initial blast, Ramsundar suffered a collapsed lung and a broken collarbone; a piece of metal the size of a playing card lodged near his aorta. Still, Ramsundar managed to make his way down nearly 30 flights of stairs. "On the 50th floor I wanted to rest, but a stranger, a guy named Doug, put his arm around me and said, 'If you can make it, let's keep going,'" said Ramsundar. "He kept telling me everything was going to be all right."

Douglas Brown, 54, a Morgan Stanley executive, was fleeing with a colleague when they encountered Ramsundar. "He had a very faraway look in his eyes," said Brown. "You noticed how many cuts were on his face." When Ramsundar said that he was bleeding badly just above the heart, Brown fashioned a compress with a handkerchief.

Outside the building Brown

Less than two hours after the second plane hit (far left), both towers had collapsed. Survivors, blanketed in ash, tried to find their way home. "When the buildings toppled," said a survivor, "it was like a volcano."

rushed Ramsundar to a medic. "A fireman gave me a compress to hold over his chest," said Brown. "I held it with my right hand and with my left hand tried to dial Silvion's wife."

Within minutes Ramsundar was whisked away to a nearby hospital as Brown rushed to escape the falling debris. On Sept. 16 the pair were reunited by phone. "It felt real good talking to him," Ramsundar said. Brown reminded his new pal of the vow he had made to buy Ramsundar a beer after the ordeal was over. Ramsundar wasn't having it. Recalled Brown: "He said, 'Nope, I'm going to buy you a beer.'"

LOUIS LESCE, 64,
A CAREER COUNSELOR

Lesce was preparing to teach a 9 a.m. class on the 86th floor of the North Tower when he felt the building shake. The ceiling caved in; thick smoke followed. He called his wife, Karen. "I thought this was it," he said. "I told her I loved her and said goodbye. I hung up real quick because I didn't want her to get emotional. I thought it might make me lose my resolve somehow."

Strangers aided Lesce—who had had a quadruple bypass—down the 86 flights. When he reached the mall beneath the World Trade Center, the South Tower collapsed. In the darkness someone grabbed him and led him through the rubble. "All of a sudden," he said, "I was outside."

Lesce found a pay phone and called Karen to tell her he was alive. As he hung up, the North Tower collapsed. Again he ran. Finding refuge in a cell-phone store, he called his wife again, telling her that he was going to the hospital.

Around 11:30 Lesce finally reached Beth Israel Medical Center. Remarkably, his only injury was a scratched cornea. For the fourth time, he called Karen—this time to tell her that he was, finally, safe.

ISABEL BURGA, 2

Watching cartoons in the family apartment in Battery Park City, Isabel Burga wasn't startled when she heard a loud boom nearby. Said her nanny, Janet Thomas, 50: "I thought it was a boat backfiring."

Minutes later, Isabel's father, Joseph, 40, a bond trader in midtown, called to tell Thomas a plane had hit the North Tower of the World Trade Center, two blocks from the apartment. He called back after a second plane hit the towers. "Get some food, pack some stuff for Isabel," Burga urged. "Go wherever you need to go, and we'll meet you."

Thomas and the little girl clutching her hand had just reached the street when the first tower collapsed, sending a multistory wave of debris cascading toward them. As they ran, a firefighter came from behind and scooped up the screaming child. Thomas was steps behind when the cloud hit; when it cleared, the child and firefighter were gone. "My God, what has happened?" a frightened Thomas thought.

At the same time, Burga and Isabel's mother, Terry Grimmig, 38, a bond saleswoman, were making their way on foot down the West Side Highway—against a tide of New Yorkers fleeing uptown—when they saw the second tower collapse. Said Grimmig: "We both started crying."

Hours later, out of leads, they returned to Grimmig's office, where they received a message that Thomas was safe but that Isabel was not with her. Burga said later, "My wife just screamed." While Grimmig's colleagues contacted police and triage centers, a PaineWebber executive e-mailed reporters he knew asking them also to be on the lookout.

It worked. Late that afternoon NBC ran a ticker at the bottom of its newscast that began, "Isabel Burga is safe." At about 6 p.m., one of Grimmig's sisters picked Isabel up at the New Jersey shelter where rescuers had taken her. "I gave her a big hug," said Susan Grimmig, "and she squished my face. It was so nice."

ARTURO AND CARMEN GRIFFITH, 54 AND 45, ELEVATOR OPERATORS AT THE TRADE CENTER

The Griffiths from the Bronx were both at their jobs in the North Tower—Arturo filling in on the freight elevator for a sick coworker, Carmen shuttling people from the 78th floor to the Windows on the World restaurant up on 106—when the first plane hit. "The elevator doors closed and I heard *bang bang*,'" said Carmen. "We were trying to get the door open." With the door half open, Carmen managed to squeeze out into a smoke-filled corridor. Just as she told her passengers it was safe to exit, a plume of fire from the elevator shaft seared her face, hands and legs.

At the same time, Arturo was knocked unconscious after his elevator plummeted at least five floors to the lobby. He came to in darkness and covered by debris. A voice asked him if he could walk. "I said yes," said Griffith. But when he tried to move, he realized his left leg was broken. As coworkers carried him outside, Arthur looked up in horror. "I saw the side of the building, and there was a big hole," he recalled. "I said, 'I want to know if my wife is okay. I don't want to lose my wife.'"

Up on the 78th floor, Carmen rolled on the carpet to extinguish the flames that threatened to engulf her. Then coworkers poured water on her burns and led her to the stairway. There, a woman she knows only as Audrey volunteered to help her. "I told her my leg is burning," she said. "She told me to put an arm on her and that she would walk me down." On the stairs Carmen began to worry about Arturo. "I said, 'My husband was on the freight elevator. What happened to the freight elevator?'" After Audrey got Carmen as far as the 20th floor, strangers carried her the rest of the way.

Taken to St. Vincent's Hospital, Arturo underwent surgery for his leg. Despite sedatives, he was awake all night: "I said, 'God, why? You should have taken me and not her.'"

Carmen, in intensive care at another hospital, asked an employee to find out if her husband had been brought in. He hadn't. Said Carmen: "I thought my husband was gone."

On Wednesday Arturo got through to his mother-in-law, who told him Carmen was badly burned but alive. On Friday they spoke by phone. "Carmen said, 'Pa, I'm okay,'" he said. "And I said, 'Ma, I'm okay.'"

JUN LEE, 37, A U.N. LAWYER

As the sky began to rain down glass and concrete, a very pregnant Jun Lee, already 10 days past her Sept. 1 due date, was looking for a way out of the concourse beneath the World Trade Center. "I didn't worry that I would go into labor," said Lee. "I just thought, 'I'm nine months pregnant, I'm going to die.'" Lee fled as quickly as she could. "People were crying, screaming," she recalled. "Cars were going against the light." She soon tired, but she knew she had to keep moving. "There was no place to stop."

About 10 blocks away at the South Street Seaport, Lee found shelter at a Best Western hotel. There she was joined at about 4 p.m. by her husband, Thomas Letsou, 41, whom she had contacted by cell phone at his midtown law office. The couple booked a room at the hotel, but by early evening it had neither electricity nor phone service. As Letsou tried to doze, Lee began to feel cramps. At midnight she poked her husband. "This is it," she said.

Through the darkened streets of lower Manhattan, the two began a gritty, two-mile, smoke-filled trek to Beth Israel Hospital, where the delivery had been scheduled. Lee's pain increased with her contractions, but, Letsou said, "she just hung in there." Eight hours later, at 1:05 p.m. on Sept. 12, Lee gave birth to 7-lb. 1-oz. Elizabeth Letsou. "She waited so long," said Lee, "and then came into this world at the worst possible time." And the best. Said Lee: "I never thought I'd be so happy to see this baby."

SHORTLY AFTER the Hutu president of Rwanda was assassinated under mysterious circumstances in the spring of 1994, long-simmering ethnic resentments erupted. Bands of Hutus murdered Tutsis—men, women and children—on sight, hacking defenseless victims to death with machetes.

In April a group of armed men arrived at the home of Paul Rusesabagina, the manager of the Mille Collines, a four-star, Belgian-owned hotel in the Rwandan capital of Kigali. Though a Hutu himself, Rusesabagina, 39, and his wife, Tatiana, 35, a Tutsi, were swept outside and piled onto a bus with 31 family members and neighbors, most of them Tutsis.

Soon the bus pulled over and the militiamen handed Rusesabagina a gun. "Their leader told me," he said, "to kill all the cockroaches," meaning the Tutsis. "I showed him an old man

SAYING NO TO A MASSACRE

Paul Rusesabagina stared down killers and saved 1,268 from slaughter in Rwanda

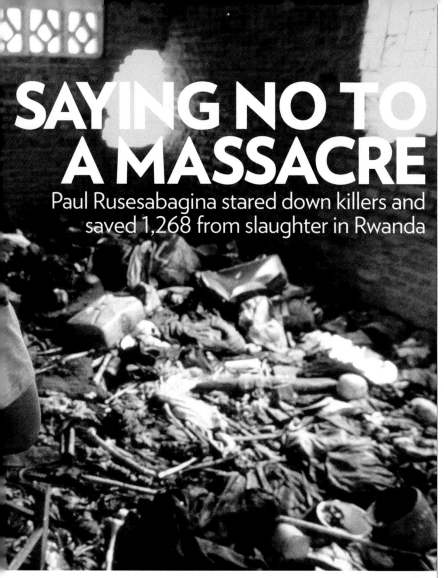

"I was just doing what every Rwandan should have done," said Rusesabagina (above) of protecting so many from the devastation. In a church in September 1994 (left), a child stood amid the bones of about 400 slaughtered Tutsis.

and said, 'Do you really believe this old man is the enemy you are fighting against? Are you sure your enemy is that baby? Take me to the hotel, and I will give you some money. But I am the only one with a key, and if you kill me, you will not have the money.'"

Two days later Rusesabagina and Tatiana moved into the hotel, bringing with them their four children and two nieces orphaned when Tatiana's brother and his wife were killed. The Mille Collines normally slept 200, but it quickly filled up with several times that number. The hotelier, who had always made it a point to hire both Tutsis and Hutus, said he never turned anyone away.

With only a few U.N. soldiers on hand to stand guard, Rusesabagina continued for more than three months to pay off the rampaging militia with the hotel's scotch and cash, and he worked every connec-

tion he had made over the years catering to the country's elite to keep his guests and himself alive. "I negotiated and juggled," he said. "If you want to control someone, it is best to keep him close to you." Added Odette Nyiramilimo, a doctor who took refuge at the hotel: "Paul had always been a very calm person and very good at his job. During the war he remained himself. He was in charge."

When the water and electricity were cut off, "my treasure was the swimming pool," Rusesabagina said. "Twice a day I would ration water out." He used the hotel's sole intact phone line to plead for help from the French, Belgian and American governments—to little avail. When refugees began to be evacuated, only foreigners were allowed out. His bosses in Belgium said they could do nothing. "They all left, but as an African I was expected to stay back and know

how to survive," he says. His voice drops slightly: "They even evacuated their dogs."

After 100 terrifying days, Rusesabagina's family and the remaining Rwandans left the hotel during a U.N.-brokered truce and made it to a refugee camp. In all, 800,000 Rwandans had perished in the carnage. Rusesabagina had wheedled, bartered and outright bribed his way into saving 1,268 fellow citizens.

When a film about his life was later proposed, Rusesabagina (living in Belgium, where he took political asylum) welcomed it. Released in 2004, *Hotel Rwanda,* he said, gave him a chance to speak to the world. His message: "What happened in Rwanda is now happening in Darfur, in the Congo—in all of these places they are butchering innocent civilians. It is high time we know that a human life in Africa is as important as a human life in the West."

CHAPTER 9

OUT OF THE PAST

PEARL HARBOR AND THE *TITANIC* WERE ONLY YESTERDAY

SURVIVING THE 'ANGEL OF DEATH'

Two friends lived after one talked Hitler's henchman, Josef Mengele, into sparing their lives

HAMBURG NATIVE Hellmuth Szprycer never knew his father, a Pole who had separated from his mother, Rosa, before Hellmuth was born. In 1938, Rosa emigrated to England, leaving 8-year-old Hellmuth and his older sisters Lotte and Gisa to be raised by her parents in a Berlin suburb that soon fell under the Nazi spell. Kids started calling Szprycer "bloody Jew," and his family was forced to wear the yellow Star of David.

The dreaded knock on the door came at 3 a.m., sometime in March 1943. Gisa, 17, was sent to work in one of the concentration camps (Lotte had died of tuberculosis), never to be heard from again, and Hellmuth and his grandparents were dispatched to the squalid Terezin ghetto near Prague. Showing his survival instinct, Szprycer, a virtuoso whistler, joined the Ghetto Swingers, a band that played in cafes for food, soap and blankets. In December, Szprycer and his grandparents were hauled off to Birkenau, a three-day trek in a frigid railway car. "In the first day 10 people died, and by the time we arrived, another 30," he recalls. It would only get worse at Birkenau, the fiefdom of one of the most notorious Nazis of all, Josef Mengele, whose cruelty and hideous genetic experiments had brought him the nickname the Angel of Death.

Shortly after their arrival, Szprycer's grandparents died, and Szprycer

He used to hide the number that had been tattooed on his arm in the Nazi concentration camp, but "now I'm more open about it," said Lowit (right, in the pink shirt with Szprycer). Selected for the gas chamber, Szprycer (left, after he was freed in 1945) walked up to Mengele and pleaded his case: "Something in me gave me power."

bonded with Harry Lowit, 13, of Prague, whose father, Karel, and mother, Milena, had run a water-proofing factory. "We had a beautiful villa on a hill," Lowit recalls. But the family's world collapsed when Karel was sent to the camp at Terezin and died. In May 1942 Harry and his mother were ordered to the ghetto, and Milena ended up in a German concentration camp. Lowit never saw her again.

For Lowit, Szprycer became a kind of big brother. The boys performed menial tasks, running errands and cleaning helmets as fellow Jews were being gassed daily in their midst. "They were crying and shouting—and then there was the smell," says Szprycer.

Periodically, a Mercedes drove into camp and Mengele would emerge. His arrival meant death: Mengele would decide which Jews would be killed and which would be spared. Those who survived would serve either as slave labor or as guinea pigs for crude surgeries in which subjects were often maimed. "He was a good-looking fella—dark, with a baby face," Szprycer said of Mengele, then 33. "You'd never have thought he was a sadist."

One day in July 1944, Mengele ordered thousands of inmates to strip and form two lines. Those sent to the right were put to work; those to the left, including Szprycer and Lowit, were bound for the gas chambers. Astonishingly, Szprycer not only stepped out of line, he approached Mengele. "I looked into his eyes," he recalled. "I clicked my heels and said, 'I want to work for you. I will do anything—clean your shoes, your motorcycle. Don't put me in the gas chamber.'" Mengele asked Szprycer where he was from. "Ah, you are a Berliner!" he barked. "Okay, I am going to [have you work at] the gate of the D-Camp."

When Szprycer returned to the others, Lowit begged him to plead his case too. Szprycer went back with Lowit looking on. This time Mengele held out two matches.

Life in Birkenau was unceasingly grim. "We all craved love," said Lowit (above, as a boy, and, right, with Szprycer). But he and Szprycer found great comfort in their friendship.

"The one who takes the longest match will live," he said. "The shortest goes to the gas chamber." Lowit came up short. "I'll never forget Harry's eyes," says Szprycer. "He cried, 'I don't want to die.'"

The intrepid young Berliner went to Mengele a third time. "What is one more?" he asked. To their surprise, Mengele relented, and the boys became messengers.

In the winter of 1944-45, the Nazis, retreating from the Russians, forced thousands of inmates from the camps to march back to Germany. Lowit eventually landed at a camp in the mountains near Salzburg, Austria. There he and a friend were made to haul coal from town in a truck. One day in April 1945, while their guards stopped for beer, the two Jews made a daring escape, driving off into the Alps. "We hid for three weeks and waited for the Americans," says Lowit.

Szprycer, who also survived what became known as the death march, made his own dash to freedom. Just before the German surrender, a gentile friend smuggled him to Prague, where he planned to board a train to France. His train was intercepted by Russian troops, who kept him under guard, but he

escaped that night on foot. When he encountered some U.S. troops along the road, Szprycer started whistling the hit American tune "Jeepers Creepers," which he recalled from his sister's records. The Americans took him in, and a regimental rabbi contacted Szprycer's mother in London. Szprycer went to Le Havre, France, with a friendly GI, stowed away on a boat to England and lived with Rosa for five years. Lowit sought him out in 1950, but thereafter they lost touch—but they never forgot.

Decades later, on Feb. 3, 1997, Szprycer, a retired antiques dealer from Ghent, Belgium, paced the marble lobby of London's Park Lane Hilton hotel. At precisely 8:30 p.m. he stopped in his tracks as Lowit, a London-based engineer, entered the atrium. Brought together by the Survivors of the Shoah Visual History Foundation, filmmaker Steven Spielberg's archive of Holocaust survivors, the friends had reunited at last. For Lowit, the reunion helped him come to terms with the past. For Szprycer, it was a celebration of their greatest triumph. "Death was on our right-hand side," he said. "But we got away with it."

BABY ON THE *TITANIC*

Nine weeks old, Millvina Dean became the disaster's youngest survivor when her father, knowing his fate, handed her over the rail

THE DEAN FAMILY was en route to a new life. Bertram, 27, had quit his job in a London pub and planned to open a tobacco shop in the American Midwest. His wife, Georgetta, in her 30s, was looking forward to raising Millvina, then 9 weeks old, and her 18-month-old brother, Bertram, in a new home they had bought sight unseen.

The liner the Deans had first booked was unable to take on fuel because of a coal strike, so the family was offered passage on the maiden voyage of the supership *Titanic*. "My father told my mother," said Millvina, "'Isn't it wonderful that we've been asked to go on the *Titanic*?'"

After the steamer struck an iceberg, Georgetta wrapped up Millvina and Bertram as warmly as possible. Then her husband escorted them to the lifeboats, staying behind knowing it would probably mean his death. "I was put in a sack because I was too small to hold," says Millvina, who was the youngest survivor of the disaster. Following two weeks in a New York City hospital, the Deans went back to England.

Destitute, Georgetta subsisted partly on money from a *Titanic* survivors fund before marrying a veterinarian. Like many survivors, she didn't recover from the 1912 disaster for years. "She went to bed with a splitting headache every afternoon," says Millvina. Nor did her mother talk much about the tragedy. Millvina, now 94, didn't even know her father had died in the disaster until she was 8 years old.

A secretary most of her life, Millvina retired in 1972 from an engineering firm in Southampton, the port from which the *Titanic* had sailed. After the release of the 1997 film *Titanic*, she was invited to finally complete her cross-Atlantic journey—this time on the *Queen Elizabeth 2*. The voyage struck no fear in her. "A lot of people ask how I like the sea," she said, "and I love it."

If the *Titanic* hadn't sunk, Dean said, "I'd be an American." After she was rescued (top), Dean, her mother, Georgetta, and her brother Bertram sailed back to England. She finally settled in New Forest, which named a street after her (above).

135

THEY REMEMBER PEARL HARBOR

American sailors and soldiers—and the Japanese pilots who tried to kill them—recall the attack that changed history

THE ATTACK BEGAN *at 7:57 on a Sunday morning. In two hellish hours, the U.S. was plunged into World War II. Fifty years after Dec. 7, 1941, the day that President Franklin Roosevelt declared would "live in infamy," American and Japanese veterans of the attack on Pearl Harbor returned to Hawaii to remember what happened and to honor the 2,403 men and women who lost their lives.*

HIRATA MATSUMURA, then 24, a Japanese torpedo bomber pilot: I had breakfast and prayed in front of the ship's shrine to do my best. Then the officers got together and heard a report on conditions at Pearl Harbor. When the meeting ended, the officers had a ceremonial toast of sake to cheer ourselves on for the attack. We raised our cups, drank and ate a few small dried fish. It was still dark outside just before 6 a.m., when I took off.

GEORGE ELLIOT, then 23, a U.S. Army private: Pvt. Joseph Lockard and I were at the radar station at the north end of Oahu. At 7:02 a.m. I was on the scope and Lockard was looking over my shoulder. We could see a blip at 137

Iyozo Fujita vowed that if his fighter was hit and crippled or ran out of fuel he would guide it into an American ship in a suicide plunge.

miles. We decided it was a large flight of planes coming in. I called in to the information center, to a fellow named Joe McDonald. He told Lt. Kermit Tyler. Tyler said to forget it—it was probably a large formation of planes from the U.S. to reinforce Hawaii.

PAT RAMSEY, then 19, a seaman on the U.S.S. *Shaw*: A Japanese torpedo plane flew over, headed toward Battleship Row. I was probably 50 feet or less from the Japanese pilot. He banked a little bit and looked out of his cockpit, and it looked like he was smiling at me.

HIRATA MATSUMURA: I saw no aircraft carriers, so we flew to the south

of Ford Island [Battleship Row] and dropped an 800-kg. torpedo from about 15 meters above the water. As we flew off to the northwest, I watched the white line my torpedo made in the water and saw the explosion it created 200 meters up in the air.

PAT RAMSEY: It looked to me like almost all of Ford Island was on fire.

JOSEPH TAUSSIG JR., then 21, an antiaircraft officer on the U.S.S. *Nevada*: I felt a very sharp blow in the bottom of my feet. Maybe 20, 30, 40 seconds after that, I felt a very sharp blow in my thigh. The ship was being strafed. I looked down, and my left foot was under my left armpit. I lost the leg.

ZENJI ABE, then 25, first lieutenant, Japanese Imperial Navy: The second wave left an hour after the first. [As we flew in] my navigator received a message by Morse code: "Tora! Tora! Tora!" ["Tiger! Tiger! Tiger!"], which meant that the surprise attack of the first wave was successful.

IYOZO FUJITA, then 24, a Japanese fighter pilot: At 9:13 a.m. we received the order "Attack!" by Morse code.

We were fighting a giant, and we believed we would lose. We didn't carry any parachutes since we intended to die.

PHILIP RASMUSSEN, then 23, an Army Air Corps fighter pilot: I strapped on my web belt and .45-cal. pistol over my pajamas, pulled on my boots and ran for the flight line. Outside the barracks, small date palms had recently been planted, and I hid behind a 3-ft. one, taking shots at the planes.

JAMES PRYOR, then 21, a private first class, Army Air Corps: When they flew over, I was just outside a hangar [at Hickam Field]. We all heard and saw the planes flying over Battleship Row. Almost instantly we saw them coming from the opposite direction, real low, along our hangar line. They were dropping bombs. We all ran and scattered. I got just into the hangar when those big hangar doors were blown out. The bomb must have come through the roof. There were several explosions. One of them tore my right hand off.

ZENJI ABE: My target that day was supposed to be an aircraft carrier in

Iyozo Fujita (far left, circa 1941) was surprised he survived the attack. The U.S.S. *West Virginia* (left), in flames on Battleship Row, was not so fortunate.

Rasmussen (left) filled several pages of his diary with his account; Geisler (center) refused for years to discuss the battle; Laughlin (right) kept shrapnel fragments as grim reminders.

> "We all ran and scattered. I got just into the hangar when those big hangar doors were blown out. The bomb must have come through the roof. There were several explosions. One of them tore my right hand off"

the harbor, either the *Enterprise* or the *Lexington*. But neither was there at the time of the attack. I was very disappointed by this, and we had to turn to attacking a battleship. Later, I found out the ship I attacked was the U.S.S. *Arizona*.

ROY JOHNSON, then 21, a navigator's assistant on the U.S.S. *Nevada*: The *Arizona* blew up 50 feet ahead of us. It was the biggest, blackest, loudest noise I've heard in my life. The ship split in two and emitted raging fires and explosions.

CLYDE COMBS, then 19, a seaman first class on the U.S.S. *Arizona*: A bomb hit turret 4 and bounced off and went down an open provisions hatch. All our doors, hatches, everything, were open. This thing went off, probably on the fourth deck. It tore things up something terrible. All the lights went out. You couldn't breathe. There was smoke in there. The feeling you got was helplessness.

PHILIP RASMUSSEN: I ran down to the hangar line and it was chaos. Ammunition was exploding in the hangars. Fires everywhere. An airplane would explode and in turn ignite the plane next to it. The only planes not burning were a few Curtis P-36s. I jumped into one and got it started. During a lull in the attack, we took off in formation. At about 9,000 feet we spotted some planes and dove to attack them.

IYOZO FUJITA: A P-36 [Rasmussen's] started attacking my plane. It was so close I couldn't get away. So I decided to die. I approached the P-36 to crash my plane into it, but then suddenly it flew away from me. I thought maybe I had hit it and it had gone down, but much later I heard the pilot of that plane is still alive, that it had landed and 500 bullet holes were found in it.

ELMER LAUGHLIN, then 21, a patrol plane pilot: Our ground and flight crews pulled machine-gun repair benches out, set up machine guns and fired away. I was standing at the southeast corner of the hangar, next to a photographer, and we watched this dive bomber come down. It hit the U.S.S. *Shaw*.

PAT RAMSEY: It was the biggest explosion you can imagine. Fire rolled over the top of the dry dock [where the *Shaw* was moored]. My feet and both my arms were burned by the flash. I must have been bending over, because my jacket rode up in the back, and I had a solid burn across my back. The shore was 50 or 100 feet away. Not far. But there was oil all over the water, and some of it was burning. We had to dive under the patches of burning oil several times. We got out and we just started walking toward where we thought the hospital was.

MARY LOUISE LAAGER GEISLER, then 23, an Army nurse: I walked out to the front where the nurses' desk was and looked down that long hall. As far as I could see there were litters with patients dying, some already dead. One young man said he was 17 and had just gone into the Navy. Then he said, "I just graduated from high school." I think he knew he wasn't going to make it, because he was bleeding from every place. It was awful, and he said to me, "Will you take my graduation ring off and see to it my family gets it?" This is the only time that day I cried.

IYOZO FUJITA: We flew back to the *Sohryu*. The mood on board the ship was happy. Of the 377 planes sent out that day, only 29 had not returned.

HARRY LONGERICH, then 24, an Army radio operator: Pearl Harbor galvanized the United States. Three or four months after Pearl Harbor, the U.S. was welded into one great country. That's what made us win the war.

THINGS WERE GOING well for Salamo Arouch. When he was a child, his father, a stevedore from Salonika, Greece, taught him how to box, and by 17, Salamo had fought his way to the light-middle-weight championship of the Balkans. Talented and young, he seemed destined for greatness. Then, in 1943, the Nazis occupied his town.

His family and neighbors were herded into boxcars and hauled like livestock to Poland and the concentration camps at Auschwitz and Birkenau. At journey's end, he said, "I saw a friend who had arrived before me. 'Where are the others?' I asked. He said, 'They are dead. All gassed and burned.' We thought he was crazy."

After Arouch was hosed down, his body shaved and his forearm tattooed with an ID number, he was taken to the center of the camp, where a brawny SS officer asked if there were any boxers among the new arrivals. Pushed forward by friends, the 5'6" Arouch was inspected by the commandant, who demanded, "Are you willing to fight right now?"

"I was exhausted from being up all night and not eating," recalled Arouch, "but I said yes."

He fought a hapless Pole and won, but his trials were far from over. Until he was freed in 1945, he triumphed roughly 200 times in the ring. Yet there was no pride in what he did: The Nazis seemed to care more for the brutality than the sport. The rules at the matches, often preceded by juggling Gypsies and dancing dogs, were always the same: "We fought until one went down or they got sick of watching," said Arouch. "They wouldn't leave until they saw blood."

Bunking with a dozen other fighters whose ranks were periodically thinned to make way for fresher, stronger men, Arouch was given extra rations and lightened work details as "compensation" for his wins. Yet there was a stronger incentive for fighting well. "The loser would be badly weakened," he says. "And the Nazis shot the weak."

Arouch later recalled Auschwitz as a living hell, saying, "Prisoners were constantly beaten with sand-filled rubber hoses and forced to work in the snow with the flimsiest clothing. Many were Poles who had lived nearby. When they tried to escape, the SS hunted them down with dogs and hung them where everyone would see." So inhuman were the conditions, he says, that "to each other, we never said 'Good night.' Only 'Sleep.' For many, it was better to be dead than to endure another day of suffering."

On Jan. 17, 1945, 10 days before the liberating Soviet Army arrived, Auschwitz was evacuated. Several months later, looking for relatives at newly liberated Bergen-Belsen, Arouch found instead 17-year-old Marta Yechiel, also from Salonika, who had barely survived a severe beating by a Nazi guard. Arouch nursed her back to health, emigrated to Israel with her and, that November, made her his wife.

Years later, Arouch attended a screening of the 1989 film *Triumph of the Spirit*—the story of Arouch himself. Despite the painful memories, he said the film brought him a kind of peaceful resolution: "I am sure I had moments when I wanted to die. But being here now to tell what happened makes me feel good about being alive."

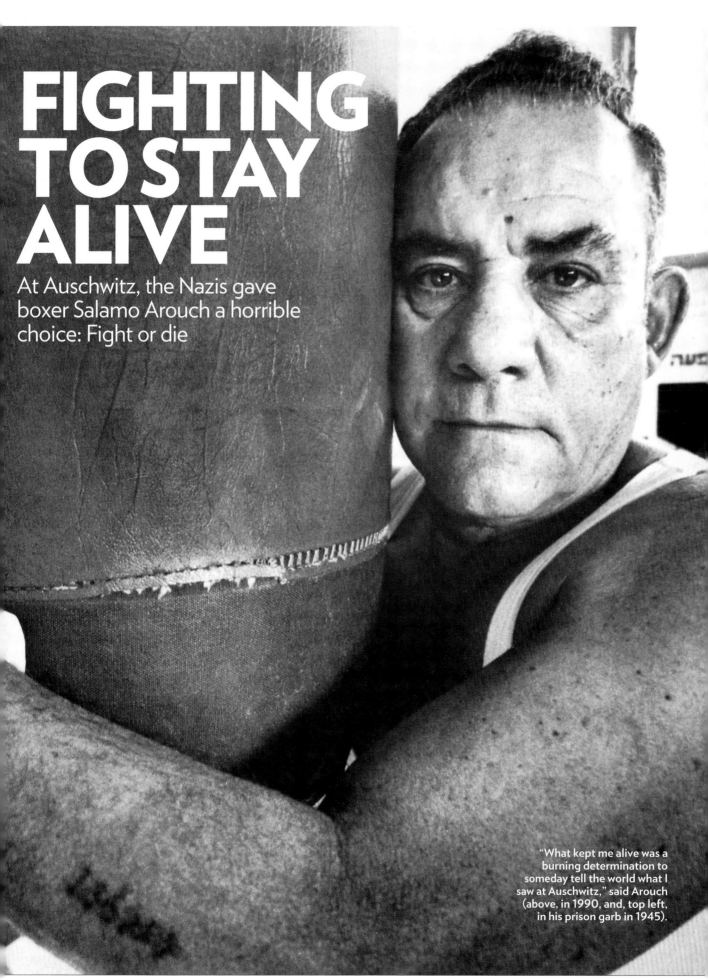

FIGHTING TO STAY ALIVE

At Auschwitz, the Nazis gave boxer Salamo Arouch a horrible choice: Fight or die

"What kept me alive was a burning determination to someday tell the world what I saw at Auschwitz," said Arouch (above, in 1990, and, top left, in his prison garb in 1945).

A MUTT THE MATCH OF ANY MAN

DOSHA THE WONDER DOG

Nine lives is not enough: Hit by a car, shot and frozen, Dosha refused to roll over

EVERY DOG HAS ITS DAY. For Dosha, a 10-month-old pit bull mix, April 15, 2003, was emphatically, definitely, positively not it. Things got off to a bad start in the morning when Dosha's owner, Louetta Mallard, 40, let her out of the house in Clearlake, Calif. Bored with the front yard, Dosha jumped over a 4-ft. cyclone fence. On the other side, unfortunately, was a road. And a fast-moving pickup truck. Dosha went down. "She wasn't moving and was glassy-eyed," said a neighbor who appeared on the scene after the accident. "I said to myself, 'That's a dead dog.'"

A Clearlake police officer arrived and, realizing there was no hope, shot Dosha in the head to end any possible suffering.

Then a public works employee took her to the local animal-control center, where she was placed in a freezer for animal corpses awaiting disposal.

Two hours later, Dosha's luck changed. A worker opened the freezer door by chance and "found Dosha sitting up," said Lake County's Animal Control director Denise Johnson. "She was alive."

According to veterinarian Debra Sally, who treated Dosha for hypothermia as well as for the gunshot wound, the bullet traveled along Dosha's skull—barely missing her brain—and settled in the skin under her jaw. Suffering hearing loss in her right ear, Dosha was released from the Clearlake Veterinary Clinic, where she vigorously licked visitors' hands. "That dog had everything go wrong, but someone was looking out for her," said Johnson. "This was her lucky day."

"It's amazing what things animals can stand," vet Debra Sally said of Dosha, who cheated death three times in one day.

CREDITS

COVER (clockwise from top left) Aperture Films/Zuma; Jonas Karlsson/Sports Illustrated; Cindy Burnham/Nautilus Productions; Steven K. Doi/Zuma

BACK COVER (clockwise from top left) Daryl Balfour/Getty; Steven Hunt/Getty; courtesy Siegfried and Roy; Rick Wilking/Reuters/Corbis

CONTENTS 2-3 Ian McKinnell/Getty

THAT'S INCREDIBLE 4 Bill Stevenson/Outdoor Collection/Aurora; **6-7** (left) Michael C. Klesius/National Geographic/Getty; Neal Beidleman/Woodfin Camp; **8** (top) Scott Fischer/Woodfin Camp; Caroline Mackenzie/Woodfin Camp; **9** (left) Bill Janscha/AP; James McGoon; **10** James Watt/Animals Animals; **11** Greg Miller; **12-13** (clockwise from bottom right) AP; Angela Rowlings/AP; Wendy Maeda/The Boston Globe (4); John Blanding/The Boston Globe; **14-15** Danny Turner; **16-17** (clockwise from bottom left) Robin Platzer/Twin Images; Guillaume Bonn/AP; Daryl Balfour/Getty; **18** Peter Tunney; **19** Peter Beard/Art + Commerce (3); **20** George D. Lepp/Corbis; **21** courtesy Hjelle family; **22-23** (left) J. Jackson Howell Photography; Ben Van Hook; (inset) Terry Parlier; **24-25** (left) Pat Kenaley; Rich Frishman; **26** Dennis Garrels/Corbis; **27** (top) The Sioux City Journal; Gary Anderson/The Sioux City Journal/Zuma; **28-31** William Campbell (3); **32-33** Guy Motil/Corbis; (inset) Rick Maiman/Polaris; **34** Marianne Barcellona; **35** Illustration by Chris Natarlle

NATURAL DISASTERS 36 Steven Hunt/Getty; **38-39** Irwin Thompson/The Dallas Morning News; **40-41** (from left) Rick Wilking/Reuters/Corbis; M. Scott Mahaskey/Army Times/AP; William Colgin/The Press-Register/AP; **42-43** Suzanne Plunkett/AP; **44** Hellmut Issels/Icon/Newspix; **45** Benjamin Lowy/Corbis; **46** Lisa Rudy Hoke/Black Star; **47** Grady County Sheriff's Dept.; **48-49** Acey Harper (2); **50-51** (left) Corbis; Eric O'Connell

CRASHES & SHIPWRECKS 52 EPA/Landov; **54-55** (left) Rick McFarland/Arkansas Democrat Gazette/Corbis; Judy DeHaas; **56-57** (top) Peter Pao/Getty/Newscom; Thomas Michael Alleman; **58-59** (clockwise from top) Reuters/Corbis; Dimis Argyropoulos/Sipa; Yannis Kontos/Corbis Sygma; **60-61** (clockwise from top left) Wade Spees; Alan Hawes/The Post and Courier; Seaman Eric Suter/United States Coast Guard/AP; William Sanders; courtesy Katadyn; **62** Jeff Riedel/Contour; **63** Jim Spellman/Ipol/Globe; **64-67** Peter Serling (5)

ADVENTURERS 68 Chris Falkenstein/Getty; **70-71** Ian Mainsbridge/Nokia/Sipa; **72-73** (from left) Michael Amendolia; Ian Mainsbridge/Nokia/Sipa; Grant Turner/Newspix; **74** Coral von Zumwalt;

75 Jeffery Salter/Redux; **76** Beth Wald/Aurora; **77** Illustration by Jason Lee; **78-79** Noah Hamilton; **80-81** (left) Jeremy Sutton-Hibbert/IFC Films; Simon Yates; **82-83** (left) Neal Preston/Retna; Barry Staver

ACCIDENTS 84 Tommy Flynn/Getty; **86-87** (left) Dan Davidson/Polaris; CJ Gunther/Reuters; **88** WPRI/CNN/Getty; **89** Will McIntyre; **90-91** (left) courtesy Siegfried and Roy; Jeff Klein/Zuma; **92** DPA/Abaca; **93** (top) Ethan Miller/Reuters, Dan Bucher/Tabloid City; **94** Dallas/Bagby/Sipa; **95** Diana Walker/Time Life Pictures/Getty; **96-97** Marian Little; **98** Mark Sennet; **99** Matthias Clamer/Stockland Martel

FIGHTING BACK 100 Adri Berger/Getty; **102-103** David McNew/Getty; **104** Dana Fineman/Vistalux; **105** (top) California Department of Corrections/AP; Casey Christie/The Bakersfield Californian/Corbis Sygma; **106** April Saul; **107** Paul Vathis/AP

MEDICAL MIRACLES 108 Chad Baker/Getty; **110-111** (left) R. Jerome Ferraro; Michelle Litvin; **112-113** Jean Paul Pelissier/Reuters; (inset) Olivier Hoslet/EPA/Landov; **114** Linda Armstrong Kelly/Sports Illustrated; **115** Jim McHugh/Corbis Outline

WORLD OF WAR 116 Paula Bronstein/Getty; **118-119** (left) courtesy Brian Alaniz and Eric Alva; Matthew Mahon; **120** Jason Dewey; **121** courtesy Brian Alaniz and Eric Alva; **122-123** Dale Wittner (2); **124-125** Robert A. Cumins/Black Star; **126** Carmen Taylor/KHBS/KHOG-TV/AP (2); **127** Gulnara Samoilova/AP; **128-129** (left) Scott Peterson/Liaison/Getty; Yves Dethler & Olivia Droeshaut/Reporters

OUT OF THE PAST 130 Brown Brothers; **132-134** Robert Wallis/Corbis (4); **135** Ian Cook (2); **136-137** Noboru Hashimoto/Corbis Sygma; **138** (top) Noboru Hashimoto/Corbis Sygma; Department of Defense; **139** (from left) Acey Harper; Zigy Kaluzny; Acey Harper; **140-141** (left) courtesy Arouch family; Rina Castelnuovo Hollander

A HUTT THE MATCH OF ANY MAN **143** Acey Harper

END PAPERS Electronic light sticks: courtesy Kriana Corp.; canteen: courtesy Armed Forces Outfitters, Inc.; scissors: Comstock; lighter and emergency water packets: Equipped to Survive; bottled water: Susanna Price/Getty; magnifying glass: Steve Gorton/Getty; whistle: Matthias Kulka/zefa/Corbis; safety pin: Christopher Stevenson/zefa/Corbis; batteries: Bernard Annebicque/Corbis Sygma; all other survival gear: Corbis (17)

Editor Cutler Durkee **Creative Director** Rina Migliaccio **Art Directors** Greg Monfries, Dragos Lemnei **Senior Editor** Rob Howe **Picture Editor** Donna Tsufura **Writer** Steve Dougherty **Research Editor** Molly Lopez **Reporters** Mary Hart (Chief), Lisa Helem, Olivia Abel, David Cobb-Craig, Paula Kashtan, Hugh McCarten, Lesley Messer, Ellen Shapiro, Ashley Williams, Jennifer Wren **Copy Editors** Lance Kaplan, Ben Harte, Alan Levine, Joanann Scali **Production Artists** Michael Aponte, Nora Cassar, Denise Doran, Ivy Lee, Michelle Lockhart, Cynthia Miele, Daniel Neuburger

Special thanks to Robert Britton, Jane Bealer, Sal Covarrúbias, Margery Frohlinger, Charles Nelson, Susan Radlauer, Annette Rusin, Ean Sheehy, Jack Styczynski, Céline Wojtala, Patrick Yang

TIME INC. HOME ENTERTAINMENT Publisher Richard Fraiman **Executive Director, Marketing Services** Carol Pittard **Director, Retail & Special Sales** Tom Mifsud **Marketing Director, Branded Businesses** Swati Rao **Director, New Product Development** Peter Harper **Financial Director** Steven Sandonato **Assistant General Counsel** Dasha Smith Dwin **Prepress Manager** Emily Rabin **Marketing Manager** Laura Adam **Book Production Manager** Suzanne Janso **Associate Prepress Manager** Anne-Michelle Gallero

Special thanks to Bozena Bannett, Alexandra Bliss, Glenn Buonocore, Robert Marasco, Brooke McGuire, Jonathan Polsky, Chavaughn Raines, Ilene Schreider, Adriana Tierno, Britney Williams